PRAISE FOR BOOKS FROM THE PLANNING SHOP

"User-friendly and exhaustive … highly recommended. Abrams' book works because she tirelessly researched the subject. Most how-to books on entrepreneurship aren't worth a dime; among the thousands of small business titles, Abrams' [is an] exception."

> —*Forbes*

"There are plenty of decent business-plan guides out there, but Abrams' was a cut above the others I saw. *The Successful Business Plan* won points with me because it was thorough and well organized, with handy worksheets and good quotes. Also, Abrams does a better job than most at explaining the business plan as a planning tool rather than a formulaic exercise. Well done."

> —*Inc.*

"Abrams' book offers a complete approach to creating your plan. Surrounding her explanatory material with commentary from top CEOs, venture capitalists, and business owners, Abrams helps you see your idea through the eyes of potential investors. Her book and your idea deserve each other."

> —*Home Office Computing*

"This book stands head and shoulders above all other business plan books, and is the perfect choice for the beginner and the experienced business professional. Rhonda Abrams turns writing a professional, effective business plan into a journey of discovery about your business."

> —*BizCountry*

"If you'd like something that goes beyond the mere construction of your plan and is more fun to use, try *The Successful Business Plan: Secrets & Strategies*, by Rhonda Abrams … this book can take the pain out of the process."

> —*Small Business School, PBS television show*

"I would not use any other book for my course on Business Development. *The Successful Business Plan* is the best I've ever seen, read, or used in a classroom environment."

> —*Professor David Gotaskie,*
> *Community College of Allegheny County, Pittsburgh, PA*

i

Successful Business Research

Straight to the Numbers You Need—Fast!

**The Planning Shop
with Rhonda Abrams**

the**Planning**shop

Palo Alto, California

ISBN 13: 978-0974-08013-0
ISBN: 0-9740801-3-6
PCN: 2006903355

Managing Editor: Maggie Canon
Project Editor: Mireille Majoor
Cover and interior design: Diana Van Winkle, Arthur Wait

Services for our readers:

Colleges, business schools, corporate purchasing:
The Planning Shop offers special discounts and supplemental materials for universities, business schools, and corporate training. Contact:

> info@PlanningShop.com
> or call 650-289-9120

Free business tips and information:
To receive The Planning Shop's free email newsletter on starting and growing a successful business, sign up at: *www.PlanningShop.com*.

> The Planning Shop™
> 555 Bryant Street, #180
> Palo Alto, CA 94301 USA
> 650-289-9120
>
> Fax: 650-289-9125
> Email: info@PlanningShop.com
> *www.PlanningShop.com*

The Planning Shop™ is a division of Rhonda, Inc., a California corporation.

"This publication is designed to provide accurate and authoritative information in regard to the subject matter covered. It is sold with the understanding that the publisher and author are not engaged in rendering legal, accounting, or other professional services. If legal advice or other expert assistance is required, seek the services of a competent professional."

> *— from a Declaration of Principles, jointly adopted by a committee*
> *of the American Bar Association and a committee of publishers*

Printed in Canada

10 9 8 7 6 5 4 3 2

NEED NUMBERS FAST? THIS BOOK IS FOR YOU!

If you're starting, running, or growing a business, you need numbers.

You need numbers to:

- Develop a successful, workable business plan

- Raise money from investors or lenders

- Find and evaluate new customers and markets

- Identify and understand competitors

- Present a convincing marketing plan to company managers

- Support the conclusions of a business plan or project for a class or competition

- Determine whether to start a company—or change a career—in a particular industry

- Make sound business decisions

Successful Business Research takes you straight to the numbers you need—*fast!*

Successful Business Research saves you time. A team of professionals, including business and marketing planning experts and seasoned reference librarians, has brought together the very best strategies and resources for finding critical business information. You'll discover how to locate the information you need in a hurry.

Successful Business Research saves you money. This book features the best *free* resources for business data. With an Internet connection, a library card, and *Successful Business Research*, you'll be able to uncover vital business information—for free. And if you have access to a college or university library, you'll find numerous other resources detailed in this book available to you at no charge!

Successful Business Research shows you exactly where to find what you're looking for—from industry growth rates and population projections to studies on consumer behavior and much, much more.

When you've got to have information *now*, *Successful Business Research* takes you straight to the numbers you need—fast!

ADVISORS & CONTRIBUTORS

This book would not have been possible without the invaluable assistance of numerous business research librarians.

In particular, The Planning Shop would like to thank the following for their thoughtful and careful guidance and for suggesting and reviewing research resources recommended in this book:

Paul Reist, Manager of Research Services

Stanford Graduate School of Business, Jackson Library
Palo Alto, California

The Jackson Library serves the needs of the students and faculty at the Stanford Graduate School of Business, one of the nation's foremost business schools. Paul Reist provided access to Stanford's collection of more than half a million business resources, expertly guided The Planning Shop's researchers through the Jackson Library's impressive collections, identified appropriate resources, and then reviewed the selected resources and portions of the manuscript. Reist, who has been at Stanford for sixteen years, previously served as a corporate librarian for Bank of America and the *San Francisco Chronicle*. He received his MLIS from the University of California, Berkeley.

Sam Richter, President

James J. Hill Reference Library
St. Paul, Minnesota

The James J. Hill Library is an independent, non-profit organization, housing a world-class collection of practical business information. It is considered one of the most comprehensive business libraries in the country. The Hill Library offers affordable memberships to individuals and businesses. The Library's dynamic president, Sam Richter, provided The Planning Shop's researchers with access to the library and assisted them in working with the collection's research librarians.

In addition, The Planning Shop would like to thank the following editorial researchers, who spent hundreds of hours in libraries and on the Internet, plowing through data, interviewing business librarians, and making certain that this book provides readers with the best business resources available:

- Julie Vallone
- Vanessa Richardson
- Veronica Adams

ABOUT THE PLANNING SHOP

The Planning Shop, located in Palo Alto, California, specializes in creating business resources for entrepreneurs. The Planning Shop's books and other products are based on years of real-world experience and share secrets and strategies from entrepreneurs, CEOs, investors, lenders, and seasoned business experts. Entrepreneurs have used The Planning Shop's products to launch, run, and expand businesses in every industry.

The Planning Shop's flagship product, *The Successful Business Plan: Secrets & Strategies,* has sold over 600,000 copies. It was acclaimed by *Forbes* and *Inc.* magazines as one of the top ten business books for entrepreneurs.

The Planning Shop's books have been adopted at more than four hundred business schools, colleges, and universities. Tens of thousands of MBA and other business students have used The Planning Shop's books and electronic templates to create business plans and enter business plan competitions.

The Planning Shop's expanding line of business books includes:

- The **Successful Business series**, assisting entrepreneurs and business students in planning and growing businesses. Titles include *Six-Week Start-Up*, *What Business Should I Start?*, and *The Owner's Manual for Small Business*.

- The **In A Day series**, enabling entrepreneurs to tackle a critical business task and "Get it done right, get it done fast."™ Titles include *Business Plan In A Day*, *Winning Presentation In A Day*, and *Finding an Angel Investor In A Day*.

- The **Better Business Bureau series**, helping entrepreneurs and consumers successfully make serious financial decisions. Titles include *Buying a Franchise*, *Buying a Home*, and *Starting an eBay Business*.

Entrepreneurs worldwide have used The Planning Shop's products to guide their business development. The Planning Shop books have been translated into Chinese, Arabic, Dutch, Vietnamese, Korean, Japanese, Czech, and many other languages.

At The Planning Shop, now and in the future, you'll find a range of business resources. Learn more at: *www.PlanningShop.com*.

ABOUT RHONDA ABRAMS

Rhonda Abrams is passionate about entrepreneurship and business planning. She writes about it, researches it, lives it. Rhonda writes the nation's most widely circulated column on entrepreneurship and small business. Successful Business Strategies appears in USAToday.com and Inc.com, as well as more than one hundred newspapers, reaching more than ten million readers each week.

The author of numerous books on entrepreneurship, Rhonda has had three books appear on Bookscan's Top 50 Business Bestseller list. Her first book, *The Successful Business Plan: Secrets & Strategies*, has sold more than 600,000 copies.

An experienced entrepreneur, Rhonda has started three successful companies, including a business planning consulting firm. Her experience gives her a real-life understanding of the challenges facing entrepreneurs. Having developed hundreds of business plans, Rhonda understands the importance of business research—finding the information and data to both make informed decisions and present a convincing plan to funding sources.

Rhonda's depth of knowledge, enthusiasm, and dynamic style have made her a frequent guest on TV and radio, and have kept her in demand as a keynote speaker for conferences and meetings. Her clients have included American Express, AT&T, Sony Music, Chevron, Hewlett Packard, Firestone, and Intuit. She has given major addresses at national conferences of the Council of Better Business Bureaus and the Association of Small Business Development Centers and at many leading universities.

Currently, Rhonda Abrams is the founder and CEO of The Planning Shop, a company focused on providing entrepreneurs with high-quality information and tools for developing successful businesses.

Rhonda was educated at Harvard University and UCLA. She lives in Palo Alto, California.

TABLE OF CONTENTS

PART I: Research Essentials

TABLE OF CONTENTS

PART II: The Research Process

PART III: Major Resources

PART IV: Straight to the Numbers You Need

HOW TO USE THIS BOOK

Successful Business Research: Straight to the Numbers You Need–Fast! streamlines your search for business information and data. Most business resources and databases listed in this book can be accessed over the Internet; many of them are free, especially when accessed through your public library. Others are available through college, university, or corporate libraries.

To use this book most effectively, you'll need:

■ A public library card, and/or

■ A college/university library card

■ An Internet connection

■ A credit card (if you plan to use any fee-based resources)

Successful Business Research: Straight to the Numbers You Need–Fast! is composed of four sections:

■ **Part I: Research Essentials** shows you the best ways to use public and college/ university libraries, explains the types of research you may want to conduct, and most importantly, gives you tips and tricks and search techniques that save you time and bring you directly to the information you're looking for.

■ **Part II: The Research Process** reveals the most effective strategies for conducting your research—including how to ask the right questions—and shows you how to evaluate and organize your findings for maximum impact.

■ **Part III: Major Resources** points you to many of the major resources for business data, including government resources, media websites, analyst reports, and research firms.

■ **Part IV: Straight to the Numbers You Need** brings you directly to the best *free* and fee-based resources for the business information and data you're likely to need. It's organized into the three topic areas most useful for business planning:

• Industry

• Company

• Target Market

The screen-by-screen sample searches in Part IV show you exactly how to navigate the resources to get the data you need quickly. Use this section as a guide when doing your own research.

Keep *Successful Business Research* at hand while you're on the hunt for facts and information. Links to key resources, research tips and tricks, and handy worksheets help you organize and present your data, making this an indispensable research tool. The numbers you need are out there—*Successful Business Research* takes you straight to them, *fast!*

Part I: Research Essentials

CHAPTER 1

Where Do I Get the Numbers?

Finding the right numbers is vital to business success. Imagine you're part of one of these real-life scenarios:

You're pitching an idea for a new company in front of a room full of venture capitalists. They're excited about your business concept. But then they start grilling you What's the size of your potential market? Can you prove that? What's the profit margin for other companies in the industry? How does the growth rate of this industry compare to the GDP? Who are your biggest competitors? Are you sure?

or

You're considering opening a second location of your successful Italian restaurant in one of three neighborhoods. You're undecided about which one to choose. You want to know: Which neighborhood has the most potential customers for Italian restaurants? What's the growth rate of each neighborhood? How much do the residents of each neighborhood earn? How many competing restaurants are already in each neighborhood?

or

It's Sunday night. You're working on a paper for your business class, due Monday. (You were supposed to have been working on this paper all semester.) Your professor requires you to back up any claims you make with numbers. You're a bit frantic and need to know: How do I find the statistics I need to give my paper, and my conclusions, validity … *tonight*?

Numbers are powerful. They give you information and insight essential to making the right business decisions. Numbers help you succeed.

But finding the critical business information you need can be overwhelming. Anyone who's ever written a business plan or developed a business proposal has had the same question:

"Where do I get the numbers?"

This book answers that question.

Academic and business databases, along with the Internet, can provide a wealth of business data and information. But accessing that information can be daunting. Each database has its own format, each website its own labyrinth to navigate. Even the way you conduct a search varies from one search engine or database to another.

Successful Business Research guides you directly to the data you require. More importantly, it doesn't just tell you how to find the business information you need—it *shows* you how.

To prepare this book, hundreds of hours were spent researching the very best business resources. Business librarians from leading universities were consulted. The resources gathered here are the ones most likely to produce the results you need.

In Part IV: *Straight to the Numbers You Need*, you'll be given a step-by-step guide through some of the key resources. You'll learn how to navigate them so you can find the information you want—*fast*.

The types of data you'll be able to find using the techniques and resources described in this book include:

- Market size

- Demographics

- Company revenues

- Company profits

- Company officers and managers

- Industry trends

- Company credit histories

- Historical performance

- Industry terms and jargon

- Forecasts and analysis

And much, much more.

Once you start doing business research following the guidance in this book, you might become hooked. It's amazing how much interesting information is out there. As you locate data that is truly relevant to your needs, you're likely to be drawn into the fascinating world of business research.

Getting the numbers right truly can give you insight—and an advantage—as you build a business or plan your career. One key to success in business is knowing how to find the numbers you need—and find them quickly! This book shows you how.

Free Resources

As resources were selected for this book, particular emphasis was placed on those that could be accessed easily—and for *free*. Some of these resources can be found on the Internet; all you need is a connection to the Web and directions on how to find them.

Other free information—and plenty of it—is available to anyone with a public library card. Public libraries maintain subscriptions to databases containing a surprising amount of outstanding business data. If you have a library card and an Internet connection, you can even access many of these databases remotely, from your home, office, or dorm room.

Additionally, those who have access to a college or university library will have an even broader range of resources available to them. In this book, the resources available at academic libraries are deemed to be *fee-based* because the general public cannot access them without having a subscription to the database provider's service or paying a fee—typically a hefty one. However, if you have access to a college or university library as a student, staff, or faculty member, you can use these resources at no charge.

A Word about Words

As you work through this book, and through the resources included, it's important to understand how certain terms are used.

Company: An individual business, whether incorporated or not. This could be a business that is a competitor, supplier, customer, strategic partner, or other.

Data and Information: In this book, the words *data* and *information* are used interchangeably. While *data* often implies quantitative or statistical information only, this book uses a broader definition because many research findings consist of both numerical and descriptive information. (For a discussion of qualitative versus quantitative data, see page 15.)

Database: Throughout this book, the term *database* is used to refer to any collection or compilation of data or information stored electronically. A database can store and organize information and statistics that are created and collected by others (for example, the Business and Company Resource Center, see pages 97 and 145) or it can store information collected by the compiler of the database itself (such as the U.S. Census Bureau or many private research firms).

Industry: Generally defined in this book as the collection of those businesses operating in a specific field of endeavor. An industry is more narrowly defined than an economic sector, such as manufacturing or retail. For instance, an athletic clothing manufacturer is in the apparel industry.

Source versus Resource: Throughout this book, the terms *source* and *resource* are used in specific ways:

- A **source** is the originator of data or information. For instance, a government agency or private research firm that conducts studies or collects data is a source.

- A **resource** is the place where you located that source. For instance, a business database which aggregates studies from many different sources (such as the Business & Company Resource Center, see pages 97 and 145) is a resource.

Target Market: A group of prospective customers or clients; these customers or clients can be either consumers or other businesses. A target market can be defined by geography or by other factors, such as by demographics in the case of consumers, industry in the case of a business target market, or a combination of those factors. For example, your target market could be male consumers, aged 35–65, living in Miami, Florida.

Terms as defined by the U.S. Census Bureau: U.S. Census Bureau data is widely used and easily accessible. It is useful to know how the Bureau defines a few key words:

- **Firm:** Synonymous with company. A business entity with one or more establishments (locations) under common ownership or control. Starbucks, for example, is one firm.

- **Establishment:** A single physical location of a business entity. Starbucks has hundreds of establishments.

- **Revenues:** All pre-tax money received from doing business, except for those monies collected for taxes (such as sales tax) from customers.

For more definitions, click on the link to **Glossary** at the U.S. Census Bureau's American FactFinder site: *www.factfinder.census.gov*. Be sure to check the glossaries at the individual resources you're using, if available, because definitions can vary from resource to resource.

NOTES:

CHAPTER 2

Using Libraries

Searching for business data once meant holing up in a library poring over stacks of reference books, periodicals, and paper reports in search of key pieces of information. Today, the research process has changed, and libraries have changed with the times. While you may no longer be poring over stacks of books there, libraries are still a vital source of information for any business research project. Both public and college or university libraries can provide access to a wealth of online databases containing valuable business information.

▩ Public Libraries

Your public library card may be the ticket to all the business data you need.

Before you start your research, pay a visit to your local library and talk to the reference librarian. Find out which databases your library subscribes to, and ask about how to access them from within the building or from home, work, or school. Talk to the librarian about the research you're doing and the kind of data you're looking for so they can direct you to the best sources for your search.

If you don't have time to visit your public library, you can start by going to the library's website. (You can usually find your library's website address by entering the name of your town and the words *public library* into a search engine.) Look for the link to the library's databases (which might also be called Reference Databases or Research Sources). You'll have to enter your library card number (and possibly your password) to access the system remotely.

Once you know how to enter your public library's databases, look over the resources available and check them against the resources featured in this book. Most public libraries offer access to databases from leading content suppliers, such as InfoTrac and EBSCO.

Part I: RESEARCH ESSENTIALS

■ College and University Libraries

If you're associated with a college or university, you have access to outstanding resources for doing business research through your institution's libraries. Academic libraries typically subscribe to many excellent business-oriented databases that would otherwise cost you a great deal of money to explore. In fact, most of the resources listed in this book as "fee-based" sources will cost you nothing to use—if you're an enrolled student, faculty, or staff member at an institution of higher education, from a community college to an Ivy League university. Moreover, the data in college and university databases tends to be more in-depth and more recent than information in databases available from public libraries.

Many larger colleges and universities have more than one library on campus; check to see if there's a separate business library. A business school library is likely to subscribe to a wider selection of business databases than a general library. However, even in a general college or university library, there's likely to be a good selection of business-related databases and a librarian who specializing in business subjects who can direct you to the best resources.

If you're not currently affiliated with a college or university, you may still be able to use their resources. Many academic libraries allow alumni and members of the public some form of limited access. Check with the college and university libraries in your area to see what their public access policies are.

Keep in mind, however, that the information on many of the databases that colleges and universities subscribe to is also sold—often for a large fee—to corporations and the public at large. The makers of those databases want to protect their valuable resources. So you may find that even if you're able to get public access to a university library, there may be limits on which databases you can use. And you almost certainly won't be able to get access to college databases from anywhere outside the library unless you're affiliated directly with that institution as a student, faculty or staff member.

A number of university libraries have developed research guides and other resources for entrepreneurs that you can access for free of charge online. These include:

■ Stanford Graduate School of Business, Jackson Library Research Guides:
www.gsb.stanford.edu/library/research/index.html

■ Harvard Business School, Baker Library Research Guides:
www.library.hbs.edu/guides/

■ Rensselaer at Hartford University, Cole Library Industry Data Finder:
www.rh.edu/library/industry/industry.htm

■ Rutgers University Business Research Guide:
www.libraries.rutgers.edu/rul/rr_gateway/research_guides/busi/business.shtml

■ University of Missouri Extension, Missouri Small Business Development Centers' Business Resource Library:
www.missouribusiness.net/library/

■ Yale School of Management, Yale University Library Research Guide to Business, Finance, and Management:
www.som.yale.edu/ssl/

The James J. Hill Research Library

If you don't have access to a college or university library and are seeking resources in addition to those available through your public library, check the James J. Hill Research Library: *www.jjhill.org*. This nonprofit private library is dedicated entirely to business topics, with most of its extensive resources available online. Membership is reasonably priced for individuals and provides access to a wealth of business databases, including many of the resources listed in this book.

CHAPTER 3

Types of Business Research

■ Primary versus Secondary Research

There are two basic types of research available to information seekers:

- **Primary:** Original research done by collecting data directly from research subjects (such as target customers). The U.S. Census Bureau conducts primary research when it sends out thousands of census takers to count every person in the country.

- **Secondary:** Research that relies on data collected from original researchers. This type of research often analyzes, compiles, or compares data collected by others.

This book deals with secondary research, showing you how to find and use information that has been collected by others and is already available in thousands of libraries, websites, and online databases.

Since primary research entails gathering data directly from subjects, conducting it is time-consuming and can be expensive. Because of the time and costs involved, many sources of primary research data are government agencies or private research companies (typically specializing in certain industries) that may charge substantial sums of money for the data they gather.

Primary research is often necessary when there is no other data available. It is particularly useful for gathering information from prospective customers for a new product or service. As you do your business research, look for sources that have conducted their own primary research whenever possible. This increases the chance that you'll be gathering the most accurate data.

Primary Research	Secondary Research
■ Raw data (not analyzed) collected by government agencies or research companies (for instance, U.S. Census Bureau or IRS data)	■ Reports based on analyzing and evaluating data collected by others
■ Data collected through consumer surveys, polling, focus groups, and taste tests	■ Graphs and charts created based on data collected by others
■ Financial data included in corporate annual reports	■ Compilations of data from a number of sources
■ Original reports, created by the collectors of data gathered using any of the methods above, including any tables, graphs, or charts	■ Articles based on interviewing those who conducted primary research
	■ Books that evaluate or analyze data collected by others

■ Market Research

Market research is a broad term that can encompass both primary and secondary research related to a target market. While the term *market research* is most often applied to doing original research about potential or current customers, you are engaging in market research any time you look for data about your target market. For example, you're doing market research when you look for census data about the geographic area in which you're planning to run a business or launch a product.

From a business perspective, conducting primary market research often provides critical insight into whether customers actually want your product or service. If you were introducing an organic dog food, for instance, you could do a great deal of secondary research and still not find crucial information. You could determine the number of dogs in the market, the sales figures for dog food, the sale figures for organic food, and so on. But, as famed venture capitalist Eugene Kleiner used to ask, "Will the dog eat the dog food?" The only way to find out is by putting the bowl in front of Fido. That's primary market research.

Primary market research can include:

- Surveys
- Focus groups
- Interviews
- Taste tests
- Sampling

■ Qualitative versus Quantitative Research

When conducting business research, you're going to be looking for cold, hard facts. You'll want to learn the size of your market, the historic growth rate of your industry, and the annual revenues of companies in your industry.

But you're also going to be looking for insight and analysis. You'll want to know more about why customers behave a certain way or which trends are likely to affect your industry in the future. In other words, you're going to be looking for both *quantitative* and *qualitative* information:

■ **Quantitative:** Data that is expressed by numbers. Examples of quantitative information include the total amount consumers spent on a product in a year, past growth rates of an industry, and numerical results of consumer surveys. You're more likely to find this kind of data in reports from government agencies and research companies, table-oriented databases, and consumer surveys.

■ **Qualitative:** Information that is expressed in words, not in numbers, and that is generally subjective in nature. Examples of qualitative information include experts' observations about what motivates consumers, forecasts for future industry trends, and subjective comments consumers make about a product. You're more likely to find this kind of information in news reports and articles from industry and general-interest publications (and databases of such articles) as well as some analyst reports.

You need to look for both types of information to conduct thorough business research. If, for example, you want to convince a group of investors that your business plan is sound, they're going to want to see hard numbers—quantitative data. They'll need answers to questions like: What's the size of the market? What's the growth rate of the industry? What's the market share distribution of your major competitors?

At the same time, many of the questions critical to the success of a business are qualitative, dealing with issues that are not easily described in numeric terms. Both you and any potential investors will want experts' insights into what trends are affecting the industry and are likely to have an impact on your business. You'll also want to know how customers perceive your major competitors.

Numbers add believability to a business plan or report because they reflect how the market or industry has actually behaved in the past. Numbers show you've done your homework. But there is no reliable quantitative data about the future. So you'll need qualitative information to give insight into what might happen in the years to come.

While this book promises to lead you "Straight to the Numbers," don't underestimate the value of qualitative data when conducting business research. Whether you're trying to convince investors to finance your business or writing a research paper on a particular industry, you can present a stronger, more compelling case by combining both types of information.

CHAPTER 4

Search Techniques

To find the business information you need, you'll likely comb through dozens of databases, online search engines, directories, and other resources. Learning a few easy search techniques will greatly improve the quality of the results you get and make your searches faster and more productive.

■ Keyword Search

Entering keywords or phrases into the search field (or search box) is the easiest way to begin any search through a database or search engine. The primary advantages of using keywords to search are speed and ease. You simply type in the word(s) or phrase(s) you're searching for, click a button on the screen (or hit **Enter** on your keyboard), and the keyword search function retrieves documents containing your keyword(s). When you use a business database or when you're dealing with a specific search term, such as the name of a corporation or a narrow industry segment, a keyword search may be sufficient to generate the results you're seeking.

However, in many cases a simple keyword search will often return too many search results, inappropriate results, or results that are not specific enough. This is particularly true of general search engines like Google, Yahoo, MSN, and AOL, while it is less likely to occur when using business databases.

Understanding how to refine your keyword searches will enable you to retrieve more relevant results.

Search Engine Optimization (SEO)

An entire industry has developed around helping businesses (and their products or services) appear prominently in search engine results. This practice is known as SEO, or search engine optimization. SEO specialists track the fast-changing methods, algorithms, and considerations used by search engines to rank sites on search result lists. These specialists then manipulate the content, headings, or coding on websites to enable the sites to appear higher in returned lists of search results. Be aware that the results that show up at the top of any search results list will not necessarily be the sites most relevant to your search, but rather, the ones most carefully optimized for the search engine.

■ Narrow the Terms

When using keywords to conduct searches, narrow your topic by using terms that are as specific as possible. One way to do that is to use more, rather than fewer, keywords to describe your topic.

For instance, if you're looking for information about companies that publish computer books and you enter the word *publishers* into a general search engine, you'll get results relating to all types of publishers, including those that publish magazines, software, and many other items unrelated to your search. If you enter the term *book publishers,* your results will include all types of book publishers. Entering the term *computer book publishers* is most likely to bring you results that contain information you can use.

However, as you expand the number of search terms you use, you may find you get few or no results, especially in business databases. If this happens, eliminate some of the terms to broaden the results.

Another way to narrow your topic when searching business databases is to search by the NAICS code of the industry you're interested in (for more on NAICS codes, see pages 25-27).

Using Advanced Search

Most search engines and many business databases have an **Advanced Search** feature. Using Advanced Search offers you more powerful options for locating the information you're looking for. This often provides a much more targeted result than using the basic search tools on the home page and subsequent pages.

Advanced Search allows you to narrow your search in a variety of ways, such as eliminating certain words, limiting the date range for results, specifying the language of results returned, and so on.

If you are having any difficulty locating the results you're seeking using keyword searches only, look for the Advanced Search option.

▥ Word Choice

The words you enter into a search box will affect the results you'll get. It's worth experimenting with various terms in your keyword searches, as different word choices can lead to very different results.

- **Synonyms.** Try a number of words with meanings similar to that of your original keyword to change the results you get. For example, instead of *income*, use *revenues*; instead of *company*, try *corporation*.

- **Singular or plural.** Use both versions of the same term. If you can't find *winery*, try *wineries*. (*Note:* Some sites, like Google, will automatically search for variants of words, eliminating the need for you to do this.)

- **Generic terms**. When looking for data about a class of product or service, use the generic term to describe it. For instance, if you're looking for information on music players like the iPod, try the term *MP3 players.*

- **Brand names**. When seeking information about a specific product, you can use the brand name of the product in the keyword search field. You'll find it helpful to include the name of the parent company if you know it (for example, *Apple iPod*). Brand names are useful when using business databases; however, when entered into a general search engine, brand names are likely to produce results aimed at consumers rather than business data.

- **Spelling.** A typo or misspelled word will completely alter your results. Some major search engines will prompt you on spelling variations; business databases will not. Take care to check the spelling when entering terms into keyword search boxes.

- **Case sensitivity.** In some databases and websites, searches are case sensitive. This means that capitalizing a word alters the search result you'll get. In these cases, the search term *Apple* would return a very different set of results from *apple.* Check to see whether the resource you are using is case sensitive; if so, be certain to capitalize all proper names, such as company names, and to avoid capitalizing other words.

Quotation Marks

You can use quotation marks on many search engines to set off and search for an exact phrase or grouping of words, such as a company name: "The Planning Shop," or a slogan or tagline: "Straight to the Numbers You Need."

Using quotation marks to define a phrase typically returns more relevant results for your search. However, be careful not to include too many terms within your quotation marks or you may get few or no results. If that occurs, try enclosing different parts of the term in quotation marks. To give you an indication of how this would work, here is an example of results retrieved through Google showing quotation marks used in different places around the same search words.

Keyword (with Quotation Marks Configuration)	Quality of Results
computer training industry statistics (no quotation marks)	More than 40 million pages returned; difficult to find relevant results
"computer training industry statistics"	No results returned; phrase too narrowly defined
"computer training industry" statistics	Good results
"computer training" "industry statistics"	Better results; more relevant pages returned; results lead to applicable U.S. Economic Census data

▪ Boolean Operators and Other Symbols

Boolean operators are words and symbols that can be added to your search words and phrases to help improve your search results. Boolean logic uses the words AND, OR, and NOT to filter information. Entering these words in conjunction with your keywords enables the search engine to determine whether you want to include all the keywords, exclude some terms, or allow variations of those words. Most search engines and databases use Boolean operators to assist in defining search terms. (Google uses them in a limited fashion.)

You *must* enter the words AND, OR, and NOT in upper case letters to enable them to limit or broaden your search.

Boole's Rules

Boolean operators were named after English-born 19th century mathematician George Boole. He invented Boolean algebra, a system of logic that can organize concepts, ideas, and words into sets. Boole's work was used as the basis for modern computer mathematics, and he is viewed as one of the founders of computer science, even though computers didn't exist in his day.

Boolean Operators

AND

Use AND to broaden a search. It retrieves items that contain *all* of your search terms. Most online search engines add AND as a default, searching for all terms automatically, so it is not usually necessary to include this.

If you enter: *wireless AND cable*

Your search will return results relating to wireless cable service.

NOT

Use NOT to limit the results of a search. It retrieves items that contain all your search terms *except* the one that follows NOT.

If you enter: *wireless NOT cellular*

Your search will return results relating to every kind of wireless service *except* cellular service.

QUICK**TIP**

Google and Boolean Operators

Google's search engine recognizes the Boolean operator OR but not the operators AND or NOT. Instead, Google uses the (+) and (-) symbols. Using the (+) can be particularly helpful when searching for common words that Google usually eliminates, such as *where* or *how*. If, for example, you were trying to figure out how to download podcasts, you would type *podcasts + how* into your search field. Since Google doesn't recognize NOT, you'll find it useful to use the minus sign to eliminate words you want excluded from your search.

OR

Use OR to find items containing *any* of your search terms. This allows you to enter variants of a word or phrase.

If you enter: *cable OR broadband*

Your search will return results relating to *both* cable and broadband services.

COMBINATION OF AND, OR, NOT

You can combine these words to more clearly define what you're searching for.

If you enter: *wireless AND cable OR broadband NOT cellular*

Your search will return results relating to wireless cable or broadband but eliminate results relating to wireless cellular services.

PLUS (+) SIGN

Use the plus sign (+) the same way you would the word AND. This retrieves items that contain all of the search terms. Make certain the plus sign immediately precedes the word you want to add, with no space between the sign and the word.

If you enter: *wireless +cable*

Your search will return results relating to wireless cable service.

MINUS (-) SIGN

Use the minus sign (-) the same way you would the word NOT. This eliminates terms from your search results. Make certain the minus sign immediately precedes the word you want to eliminate, with no space between the sign and the word.

If you enter: *wireless -cellular*

Your search will return results relating to every kind of wireless service *except* cellular service.

Other Symbols

Like the (+) and (-) signs, other characters and symbols can help shape your search through certain resources. These include:

* (ASTERISK)

The asterisk is considered a wildcard in most search engines and many databases. Placing an asterisk at the end of a word retrieves different forms of the word, broadening your search.

If you enter: *Italian**

Your search will return results for *Italiano, Italiana, Italianate,* and so on.

? (QUESTION MARK)

A question mark enables you to replace one or more characters in a word (one character per question mark) to find similar words.

If you enter: *wom?n*

Your search will return results for *woman* and *women.*

() (PARENTHESES)

Using parentheses to separate phrases is called *nesting* and enables you to use more complex search terms to find better results.

If you enter: *(New Orleans AND Katrina) AND (FEMA OR federal aid)*

Your search will return results that relate to *both* the city of New Orleans *and* Hurricane Katrina and that *also* contain references to *either* FEMA *or* federal aid.

~ (TILDE)

Google and some other search engines allow you to place the tilde sign (~) immediately before a word to search for synonyms.

If you enter: *~pasta*

Your search will also return results for *noodles.*

OTHER PUNCTUATION MARKS

Some search engines and databases recognize other punctuation marks, such as hyphens, apostrophes, and ampersands (&). Others don't. Try adding or eliminating those punctuation marks to see how they affect your results.

■ Additional Search Tips

Each search engine or database has its own quirks when it comes to the use of punctuation marks and other types of shortcuts. You can usually find a description of the search tools for the particular resource you're using on its home page or somewhere near the search field.

Once you have chosen your resource, take the time to review any search tips available. Moreover, since technology is constantly changing and improving, it's worth checking into the online search tips for the resources you use most often from time to time to see what's new.

QUICK**TIP**

Proximity Operators

Many databases and search engines allow you to use the terms NEAR, BEFORE, and AFTER to specify how close words should be to each other or where they should appear in relation to one another in the results. Others use this logic by default, based on your ordering of the words.

CHAPTER 5

Searching by NAICS or International Codes

■ NAICS

Every type of business in North America has been assigned a numerical code called a **NAICS** code. NAICS (pronounced *nakes*) stands for North American Industry Classification System. NAICS was developed by the governments of the U.S., Canada, and Mexico as a way to standardize industry categorization. You will often be asked to provide a NAICS code as part of a search for business information. Knowing the NAICS code for the industry you're interested in makes searching for, and finding, data about it much faster and easier and produces more accurate results.

For instance, if you were searching for data about online retailers such as Amazon.com or Overstock.com, would you look for information about technology, retail, or information businesses? Online retailers are certainly technology businesses, but they make their money in retail sales, and they also provide information. Once you know the NAICS code for this type of business (it's 454111: Electronic Shopping, by the way), you're more likely to find the right data for that industry.

If you were looking for information at the American FactFinder Quick Reports section on the website of the U.S. Census Bureau, typing in the NAICS code for the type of business you're interested in would quickly bring you to detailed industry data on that business. (See page 106 for more information on Quick Reports.)

You'll find it much easier to locate government and other information if you can type in the NAICS code when conducting searches online.

■ Understanding NAICS

NAICS divides the economy into twenty broad economic sectors (including Manu-facturing, Retail Trade, and Information). The system then further groups those broad economic sectors into subsectors, then into specific industries or business types.

Each of the twenty broad economic sectors is assigned a two-digit code. To further identify specific industries within those broad sectors, NAICS adds additional numbers.

If you owned a Harley Davidson motorcycle dealership, your dealership would fall into the six-digit NAICS classification 441221 for motorcycle dealers.

1. The first two digits refer to the broad economic sector the dealership belongs to:
   44: Retail Trade

2. A third digit is added to designate a subsector of that two-digit sector:
   441: Motor vehicle and parts dealers

3. A fourth digit refers to more specific industries or businesses within the classification:
   4412: Other motor vehicle dealers (in other words, not automobile dealers)

4. A fifth digit adds further distinctions between businesses within the classification:
   44122: Motorcycle, boat, and other motor vehicle dealers

5. Numbers with a non-zero sixth digit usually refer to very specific industries or types of businesses:
   441221: Motorcycle dealers (that is, not boat or other motor vehicle dealers)

Your economic sector might not always be immediately obvious. For instance, you might have thought that motorcycle dealers would be classified as part of Transportation and Warehousing.

Keep in mind that this is a government-designed description, and some businesses won't seem to fit within a specific industry. That's why you'll usually find an *Other* category in each sector and subsector. However, the data for *Other* may not be very relevant, as it is a catch-all for businesses that didn't fit into any other classification. For instance, "all other motor vehicle dealers" includes dealers of both snowmobiles and jet airplanes.

QUICK**TIP**

NAICS and SIC

NAICS replaced the previously used classification system, the Standard Industry Classification System (SIC), in 1997. You'll sometimes still see references to SIC codes in some databases.

CODES FOR NAICS TOP-LEVEL ECONOMIC SECTORS

Code	NAICS Sector
11	Agriculture, Forestry, Fishing and Hunting
21	Mining
22	Utilities
23	Construction
31–33	Manufacturing
42	Wholesale Trade
44–45	Retail Trade
48–49	Transportation and Warehousing
51	Information
52	Finance and Insurance
53	Real Estate and Rental and Leasing
54	Professional, Scientific, and Technical Services
55	Management of Companies and Enterprises
56	Administrative and Support and Waste Management and Remediation Services
61	Education Services
62	Health Care and Social Assistance
71	Arts, Entertainment, and Recreation
72	Accommodation and Food Services
81	Other Services (except Public Administration)
92	Public Administration

QUICK**TIP**

Finding your NAICS Code

You can get a complete list of NAICS codes at the U.S. Census Bureau's website: *www.census.gov/epcd/ naics02/naicod02.htm*. You can also do a keyword search there to find the NAICS code of the industry you're interested in.

■ International Classification Systems

When doing research on international businesses, you may find it helpful to know the industry classification codes used by the countries for which you are seeking data. The challenge: there are quite a few of these classification systems.

A few sites that will help you find the codes specific to the countries that interest you:

THE UNITED NATIONS STATISTICAL DIVISION

http://unstats.un.org/unsd/cr/ctryreg/ctrylist2.asp

This site provides descriptions of various national classifications and a chart enabling you to see which nation is using which system.

ISIC

http://unstats.un.org/unsd/cr/registry/regcst.asp?Cl=17

The International Standard Industrial Classification (ISIC) of all Economic Activities, or versions of it, is used in numerous countries throughout the world.

NACE

http://europa.eu.int/comm/competition/mergers/cases/index/nace_all.html

NACE is the classification system used to describe economic activities in the European Union.

GLOBAL INDUSTRY CLASSIFICATION STANDARD (GICS™)

www.msci.com/equity/gics.html

The Global Industry Classification Standard (GICS) was created by Morgan Stanley Capital International (MSCI) to provide standardized industry definitions for the investment community.

NOTES:

Part II: The Research Process

THE RESEARCH PROCESS

The prospect of searching dozens of Internet sites and computer databases for important facts and figures can be daunting. It doesn't have to be.

Searching for information can be easy—and rewarding—if you approach it in a systematic way. The key to successful business research is breaking down the process into a few simple steps:

- **Step One:** List the specific questions you need to have answered.

- **Step Two:** Choose the resources most likely to provide the answers you need.

- **Step Three:** Evaluate the quality and objectivity of the data you find.

- **Step Four:** Organize your data and cite it appropriately.

Follow these four steps straight to the numbers you need!

CHAPTER 6

List Your Questions

Once you begin exploring research resources, you might find yourself overwhelmed. There's a lot of information out there, but that doesn't mean that every bit of data you'll find is data you need. Moreover, as you do your research, you'll often discover that one resource or one piece of data can lead you to many other links and sources. This can be a terrific way to find what you're looking for—or it can take your time and attention away from the task at hand.

To keep focused and save time, the best way to start the research process is to be very clear about exactly what you're looking for. Begin by answering two questions:

1. What is the primary question I want my research to answer?

2. How am I going to use the information I find?

Your primary question is likely to be fairly broad, especially if you are in the early stages of your research. For instance, if you were considering opening a sporting goods store in Chandler, Arizona, your primary question would be: Is the market for sporting goods in Chandler big enough—without overwhelming competition —for me to be successful?

It's unlikely that you'd find a single resource that would answer that particular question. After all, to answer it you'd need information about the market, the competition, the sporting goods industry, and more.

To get the answer you're looking for, you must break down your broad primary question into a series of more specific questions. Answering these will give you the data you need to draw your conclusions. Some questions you could ask include:

1. What is the demographic makeup of the people in Chandler, Arizona?

2. What is the demographic makeup of people who buy sporting goods?

3. Are the Chandler demographics consistent with the demographics of sporting goods purchasers?

4. Is Chandler's population growing? By how much? Is it changing? In what ways?

5. How many sporting goods stores are there currently in Chandler?

6. How does that number compare to the number of sporting goods stores in other cities with similar population size and characteristics?

7. What are the leading sporting goods stores in Chandler?

8. Are there any national sporting goods stores that might be targeting Chandler for expansion?

9. What are the profit margins for sporting goods stores?

10. What is the growth rate of the sporting goods industry nationwide?

11. What are the important trends affecting the sporting goods industry?

Next, consider exactly how you plan to use the information you find. This will influence, to some degree, the kind of data you're seeking and how extensive your search will be. For instance, if you're looking for investors for a new company, you can expect the data in your business plan to be examined more closely than if you were looking for data for a presentation in a classroom seminar. And the consequences of presenting the wrong data to potential investors are much worse!

Some of the ways you might use research information include:

■ Creating a business plan to secure funding

■ Creating an internal business plan or strategic plan

■ Creating a business plan for academic use/competition

■ Assessing viability of starting/expanding a business

■ Assessing competitors

■ Evaluating industry trends and opportunities

■ Identifying potential customers

■ Identifying potential suppliers

■ Researching potential strategic partners

Keep your goals in mind while doing your research. This will help you focus on the data most likely to help you achieve them.

WORKSHEET: **Research Goals**

▪ What is the broad primary question you want your research to answer?

_____

_____

_____

▪ What are the more specific questions that will help you answer the primary question?

_____

_____

_____

_____

_____

_____

_____

_____

_____

_____

_____

▪ How do you plan to use the information you find? (In a business plan? Research paper? Presentation?)

_____

_____

_____

_____

_____

■ What kind of information do you need to answer your questions? (Qualitative, such analysts' insights about trends, or quantitative, such as sales figures, industry or target market growth rates?)

_____

_____

_____

_____

_____

_____

■ What geographic region do you plan to cover?

_____

_____

_____

_____

_____

_____

■ What other key factors do you need to keep in mind during your research process? (Specific concerns of investors, professor's course requirements, and so on.)

_____

_____

_____

_____

_____

_____

WORKSHEET: Research Questions

List the questions you are seeking answers for in each of the following areas. A few potential questions are listed first.

■ **Industry/Economic Sector**

• What is the size of the industry of which your business is a part?

_____

_____

• What has the growth rate of that industry been over the last few years?

_____

_____

• What is the projected future growth rate of that industry?

_____

_____

• What are the leading products/services in that industry?

_____

_____

• What are typical profit margins in that industry?

_____

_____

• What are the key trends/developments affecting that industry?

_____

_____

• Is the industry dominated by a few major companies or are there many healthy competitors?

_____

• Other:

_____

• Other:

_____

■ **Target Market**

• What are the demographic characteristics of your target customers? (That is, age, gender, marital status, income, education level, type of business, and so on.)

_____

_____

• What is the size of your potential market in actual numbers? (That is, how many people/businesses fit the characteristics of your target customers in the specific geographic location you're targeting?)

_____

_____

• What is the size of the potential market in your specific geographic area in terms of revenue?

_____

_____

• What has the growth rate of that market been over the last few years?

_____

_____

• What is the projected growth rate of that market?

_____

_____

• How many other companies in your type of business currently serve the target market?

_____

_____

• Other:

_____

_____

• Other:

_____

_____

■ **Company**

• Which companies are the leading competitors in your industry?

_____

_____

• Which companies are the leading competitors in your specific geographic target market?

_____

_____

• How is market share divided?

_____

_____

• What products/services do your leading competitors offer? At what price?

_____

_____

• How are your competitors perceived in the marketplace?

_____

_____

• Who are some potential customers for your products/services? What are the names of key personnel and their contact information?

_____

_____

• Who are some potential suppliers of products/services that you need? How do their current customers rate them?

_____

_____

• Other:

_____

• Other:

_____

CHAPTER 7

Choose Your Resources

Once you have identified the key questions that will be the focus of your research efforts, you'll want to locate the best sources for data that will answer them.

Three ways to do this efficiently are to:

- Search the resources this book

- Ask a librarian

- Use research guides

■ Search the Resources in This Book

Start by looking at the resources listed in Part IV: *Straight to the Numbers You Need*, beginning on page 87.

The resources you'll find there were selected after hundreds of hours of examining business resources and consulting business librarians. They are some of the best available for business research.

These listings are separated into three main topic areas to make your search for information easier:

■ Industry

■ Company

■ Target Market

Focus on the resources in this book related to the topic area of your research (for example, target market). But keep in mind that resources listed in one topic area are likely to be useful in others, as well.

In addition, check the "Major Resources" section beginning on page 59. It's likely that you'll be able to find much of the information you're seeking from the resources listed in *Sucessful Business Research*.

■ Ask a Librarian

Librarians are trained to assist researchers in finding the information they're looking for. Most libraries—particularly college and university libraries—employ librarians who are specifically assigned to help business researchers. These librarians are familiar with the resources in the library that can best answer your research questions. They can direct you to the appropriate resources in databases, online, and in print.

As part of your research project, plan a visit to a well-stocked library. Call ahead of time to speak with a business reference librarian and arrange to visit when the librarian will be available to assist you. Describe as specifically as possible the kinds of data you're seeking (that is, the answers you're trying to find).

You'll find that consulting with a librarian is an excellent way to improve the efficiency and success of your business research.

▣ Use Research Guides

A number of university libraries have compiled guides to assist business researchers in locating the information they need. These guides describe the resources in their libraries—resources that are likely to be found in most well-stocked libraries (especially other academic libraries). Refer to these research guides if you need additional help in finding appropriate resources. See pages 10-11 for more information and a list of research guides.

▣ Know Which Resource to Choose

Business research resources come in many forms. It helps to know what type of resource is most likely to produce the kind of results you're seeking:

■ **Online search engines.** Online search engines retrieve information from the Internet. They are particularly good for finding recent news and accessing publicly available resources, such as government agencies' databases. (For more information on search engines, see page 59-61.)

■ **Academic/Business databases.** A database is a collection of information, articles, or other records stored electronically. Academic and/or business databases store information that is particularly relevant to researchers. Databases store journal and magazine archives as well as reports from government agencies and research firms. (For more information on databases, see pages 65-68.)

■ **Government resources.** Many government agencies collect and compile data relating to the economy. These resources are particularly useful for finding statistics. Their data is generally considered reliable and conservative. (For more information on government resources, see pages 71-79.)

■ **Private research companies.** Private research companies compile data that is used by corporations and industry leaders to aid them in decision making. Their reports are good for specialized information. Since these are for-profit companies, the data can be very expensive to acquire (sometimes in the many thousands of dollars). But it may be worth it to obtain data that is particularly relevant to your needs. (For more information on private research companies, see page 68.)

Don't try to be exhaustive in your research efforts; it's not necessary or possible. Remember: you are looking for information that will answer your key questions and meet your needs. At the same time, your research must be thorough enough to give you, and those reading your plan, confidence that your data is accurate and drawn from reliable sources.

CHAPTER 8

Evaluate Your Data

Once you've collected your data, you're likely to be faced with a challenge: You now have a lot of data, perhaps more than you can actually use. How do you select the information that's most relevant, most accurate, and will best help you meet your goals?

For instance, you may find one source that says an industry is growing at 5 percent per year, another that says it's growing at 2 percent, and another claiming the industry is actually shrinking. How do you know which piece of data to trust—and use?

You've got to apply some critical analytical skills when you're evaluating the data you've collected. For every piece of information you collect, you must consider the:

■ Source

■ Time period

By the way, don't imagine that you can choose to present only the data that supports your conclusions. That's not only a bad way to make business decisions; it's also likely that an investor or professor will have access to the same data as you and will be quick to point out that things may not be as rosy as you make them seem. Prove that you've done your homework by showing the range of data available, even if it is not always as favorable as you might like. Your thoroughness and honesty will add credibility to your plan.

■ Consider the Source

Contrary to popular belief, sometimes numbers *do* lie. That's why, when evaluating data, you must always consider its source. Remember, the source is not necessarily the website or database where you found your information, but the entity that did the primary research and compiled the data you found.

One of the first things to look for when examining a data source is whether any potential bias or hidden agenda is influencing the data. Imagine that you are searching for data on cigarette sales to minors. You find several studies on the issue, drawing very different conclusions. Which source do you believe offers the most reliable data?

- A government agency

- A tobacco industry association

- An anti-smoking advocacy organization

- A private, for-profit research company

- A university research study

Any one of these sources might have an agenda other than simply reporting the facts. For instance, although both the tobacco industry association and the anti-smoking organization might have special expertise on the topic of cigarette sales, their particular points of view could lead to inherent bias in their research results. The private, for-profit research company may well be conducting the study for a client with a special interest in the issue (such as the tobacco industry), and this could also skew the results.

Remember, the types of questions a researcher asks, the size of the survey sample, the composition of those surveyed, and how the data is compiled can all dramatically influence the results produced.

Generally, the most accurate sources are considered to be:

- **Government data**, particularly from the U.S. Census Bureau. Government data is generally regarded as fairly accurate, as it is drawn from large samples. Also, it is expected that such data is free from inherent bias.

- **Private research company data.** Private research companies are paid large sums of money to gather data relating to an industry. Since their primary income comes from the sale of such data, their accuracy is directly related to their ability to stay in business.

- **Studies conducted by universities.** Generally, studies conducted by university faculty and researchers are highly regarded. Such studies typically undergo academic review and are likely to follow accepted research procedures. Ideally, such studies are relatively free of bias.

- **Studies using large samples.** The greater the number of respondents, the more likely the information they supply reflects reality.

In many situations, finding information about the method(s) used to collect data can help you evaluate its credibility. For instance, trade associations may be an excellent source of data, since many trade associations collect information about their industries. However, this data may be either highly reliable—when it comes from those associations that are careful and objective in their research—or highly unreliable—when, for example, an association uses data for political or marketing purposes.

When assessing the quality of data, look for:

GOOD SIGNS

- Data was collected by an independent research firm

- Large sample size

- Large percentage of those polled responded

- Objective, neutral questions were asked

BAD SIGNS

- Study was funded by a private company or association with a political agenda

- Small sample size

- Small percentage responding

- Questions were skewed to elicit particular responses

Data with an Agenda

Be particularly cautious when evaluating data from certain types of sources. This can include:

- Statistics from individual companies, which may have manipulated data to increase sales

- Data from politically or economically motivated organizations, which may have had a special agenda and used research techniques that support the message they want to send

- Data from studies with very small samples, which may not represent reality

■ Time Periods

If all other factors are equal, the best data is the newest. A lot can happen in even a few years, so it's generally better to present data from the last year or two, if you can find it.

A couple of exceptions exist, however. Data from the U.S. Census Bureau is always at least a couple of years old, and it is generally regarded as quality data. Because the Census Bureau collects such a large amount of data and checks it so thoroughly, there is a lag between when the data is collected and when it is made available to the public. The U.S. Economic Census is conducted every five years, and the results take a couple of years to become public, yet this data is considered to be useful and authoritative.

It's important to look not only at how recent data is but also at the time period the data covers. This can have a significant effect on the conclusions you can draw from it. For instance, here are two headlines adapted from real newspaper stories reporting on the same study:

VC funding falls to 7-year low

VC funding increases by 7 percent

Both of these headlines are completely accurate. Both reported on the same study. How could this be? Each article focused on data from different time periods in the study.

The first article focused on data for the last quarter of the year. That data showed that the total amount of venture capital funding for the quarter was the lowest in seven years. The second article reported on the total amount of funding for the entire year. Compared to the total for the year before, the amount had actually increased.

Be certain to take note of the date of the study, the time period the data was collected, and the period about which any conclusions were reached.

NOTES:

CHAPTER 9

Organize Your Data

You're going to be combing through dozens of databases and resources looking for the information you need. It's easy to lose track of where you found a particular statistic. When you're ready to prepare your business plan, proposal, or academic paper, you may discover you have no idea of the source of some of your data. This can create some very unfortunate results.

First, you may inadvertently copy others' work if you don't separate it from your own while you collect it or you don't note where it came from. Whether you intentionally or unintentionally use work written by others, it's still considered plagiarism.

Plagiarism is a serious ethical offense.

Appropriate citations are particularly important in academic papers. Plagiarism can cause you to fail a class or face disciplinary action. In the business world, plagiarism is viewed as a sign that you are untrustworthy. Potential investors or partners will avoid doing business with you if they suspect you of such behavior. Even when no one suspects you of behaving unethically, failure to keep track of your sources is sloppy—and dangerous.

Readers of business plans and other business documents will want to know the sources of the information in your work. You may be questioned about your conclusions and you need to be able to cite the sources of your data. More than one entrepreneur has had a business plan rejected by investors because they couldn't support claims about the size of their market or their potential profit margins.

To avoid these types of problems, carefully organize your findings and note sources and resources as you do your research.

As you collect data, be certain to note where you found it. You'll need this information:

- For appropriate citations (critical in academic papers)

- To defend your strategies and conclusions (especially important when presenting business plans)

- If and when you want to go back for additional information or updates from a resource

To help you keep track of your data, a worksheet is provided on page 56 for use as a guide. Keep notes—indicating the information found, source, date, and so on—as you gather information from each source. Be certain to distinguish between the originator of the data—the source—and the place you found the data—the resource—if they are different.

Sources versus Resources

When providing citations for information, it's important to distinguish between the *source* of the data and the *resource* where you found the information, if the two are different.

- A **source** is the originator of data or information. A government agency or private research firm that conducts studies and collects data is a source.

- A **resource** is the place where you located that source. A business database which aggregates studies from many different sources (such as the Business and Company Resource Center) is a resource.

■ Citation Style

Academic

There are a number of different citation styles used in academia, including:

- **MLA:** Modern Language Association (popularly used in the humanities)

- **APA:** American Psychological Association (popularly used in the social sciences)

- **CBE:** Council of Biology Editors/now the Council of Science Editors (popularly used in the sciences)

Check with your professor about the citation style appropriate for your assignments. For more information about academic citation, see the citation guidelines compiled by Duke University Libraries: *www.lib.duke.edu/libguide/cite/works_cited.htm*.

Business

Citations in business plans (particularly those produced for internal use or when seeking financing) and other business documents can generally be less formal than those used in academic papers.

One method that can be used is to cite the title of the study, source, and date in parentheses after including a statistic or excerpt from another source. For example:

There were 148 software publishers in the greater Austin/San Marcos metropolitan area in 2002 (County Business Patterns, U.S. Census Bureau, 2002).

You may also want to include a complete list of sources in the appendix to your business plan. This adds credibility to your presentation.

Tricks of the Research Trade

Whenever you cut and paste information from another source, take steps to differentiate it from your own notes or original work. You can put it in a separate computer file (noting its source), copy it in a different color, or place quotation marks around the material. Write down the source of the data, where you found it, and the date you found it *as soon as* you gather it.

WORKSHEET: Organizing Data Sources

▪ Data Found:

_____

_____

▪ Resource used to locate data (database, website, or print source):

_____

_____

▪ Location of resource (Web address, name of database, call number, or issue date):

_____

_____

▪ Original source of data (name of study):

_____

_____

▪ Original source of data (name of individual/organization originating data):

_____

_____

▪ Date data found:

_____

_____

▪ Notes/Comments:

_____

_____

Part III: Major Resources

CHAPTER 10

Search Engines and Online Directories

Two of the most useful types of resources to help you find the business data you're looking for on the Internet are search engines and online directories.

Both search engines and online directories help you retrieve information from billions of web pages, but they work in very different ways:

- **Search engines** (such as Google) rely on software programs that crawl the Internet (or search their database of stored websites) to find documents or pages containing terms requested by the user. The results they return are based on sophisticated mathematical formulas (algorithms) that determine whether a document is appropriate.

- **Online directories** (such as Yahoo's directory, which was one of the first and most popular) are organized by topic, in a hierarchical format. The choice of which topics to list a website under is usually made by humans, rather than software.

Search engines produce a greater number of results, more quickly, than online directories. However, since crafty website operators often manipulate search engine algorithms in order to get their websites to rank higher in the results, you may have to wade through a number of irrelevant—even annoying—websites to find what you're looking for.

Directories, which are constructed by human judgment, may return fewer pages or documents than search engines, and the results are often more dated. However, working your way through a directory is likely to reveal many sites related to your topic that you wouldn't otherwise have seen. Moreover, a number of specialized online directories—such as Yellow or White Pages directories—can often help you find information, such as a phone number, more quickly than search engines.

When conducting business research, it's well worth becoming familiar with the advanced features of at least one search engine and one online directory.

If you're frustrated with the results you get using a search engine or a directory, give the other type a try.

■ Search Engines

You're almost certainly familiar with search engines; you probably use one nearly every time you use the Internet. Google is by far the most popular search engine in the U.S., according to Nielsen/Net Ratings. Nearly half of all online searches are conducted on Google.

The next three most-used search engines are:

- Yahoo!: *www.yahoo.com*

- MSN: *www.msn.com*

- AOL: *www.aol.com*

Using search engines is relatively easy. All search engines have clearly visible search boxes on their home pages--just type in your keywords or phrases, press the search button or **Enter** on your keyboard and pages of results will appear on your screen. To improve your results, refer to the *Search Techniques* section on pages 17-23.

It's also worth becoming familiar with the specific features of the search engine you use most often. For instance, Google does not recognize Boolean search operators (for more on Boolean operators, see pages 21-22), while other engines do. So entering the words *The Planning NOT Shop* on Google still provides a result including The Planning Shop, while doing the same search at MSN excludes pages from The Planning Shop.

Remember, however, that search engines rely on software and algorithms to rank a website. No humans have looked to see whether a site--or the information it contains--is trustworthy. A healthy dose of skepticism comes in handy when assessing information from any website. Use your evaluative skills (see pages 47-50) to judge how much credibility to give any data you gather from websites.

Google

Google is the most-used search engine in the U.S., but there's more to Google than what's immediately visible on the home page. You can find many additional resources for business research by using some of Google's specialized search engines:

GOOGLE NEWS

http://news.google.com/

Searches thousands of news sources. Faster than the general Google search engine when searching for recent developments about a company, newly released government data, or other recent developments.

QUICK**TIP**

Advanced Search

Be certain to explore the Advanced Search option on the search engine you use most. Using it increases the chance of getting the most relevant results for the information you're seeking.

GOOGLE IMAGE

www.google.com/imghp

Searches the web for photos, graphics, illustrations, and logos.

GOOGLE SCHOLAR

http://scholar.google.com/

Searches academic journals and papers.

GOOGLE BOOKS

http://books.google.com

Searches the content of selected books.

Yahoo!

YAHOO! FINANCE

http://finance.yahoo.com

Locates stock-market-related information on companies as well as company news from such sources as Reuters, Business Wire, Associated Press, and Motley Fool. (For more on Yahoo! Finance, see page 171.)

YAHOO! AUDIO

http://audio.search.yahoo.com

Searches general and business audio content, including interviews and podcasts.

MSN

ENCARTA

http://search.msn.com/encarta/results.aspx?FORM=MSNH&q=

Clicking on the **Encarta** link at the top of the MSN home page or entering the URL above will bring you limited-time access to the Microsoft Encarta Online encyclopedia.

AOL

AUDIO

http://search.aol.com/aol.com/audiohome

Searches general and business audio content, including interviews and archived radio broadcasts.

QUICK**TIP**
Metasites

Instead of conducting their own searches of the Internet, metasites search the results of other search engines simultaneously and return all of them to you. Three to try:

■ **Clusty:** *www.clusty.com*

■ **Dogpile:** *www.dogpile.com*

■ **Kartoo:** *www.kartoo.com*

■ Online Directories

Internet directories are organized hierarchically: you start from a broad category, then click through to subcategories of that category, continually narrowing your search until you arrive at the links you need. For instance, on the main page of a directory, one option is likely to be *Business*. Once you click on that, you'll be presented with a list of various topics relating to business. Let's say you select *Marketing*. Click on that and you'll be presented with a list of marketing topics. You might then click on *Advertising*. You'll then see another list of categories limited to advertising, and so on.

This hierarchical format enables you to narrow in on exactly what you're looking for. It's not only a good way of finding information, but it can give you ideas about other topics closely related to your search topic (and other terms that can be used to find what you're looking for). Directories are especially useful if you're trying to find a vendor, since many online directories are oriented towards sales.

General Online Directories

YAHOO! DIRECTORY

http://dir.yahoo.com/

Yahoo! was the first widely popular Internet directory. However, commercial sites must now pay to get listed in Yahoo's directory, which limits the results returned.

DMOZ

www.dmoz.org

The Open Directory Project produces what they claim to be the "largest, most comprehensive human-edited directory of the web." Websites do not need to pay to be listed in this directory. The ODP also operates the directories for many other search engines and portals, including Google's directory (*www.google.com/dirhp*), AOLSearch, Netscape Search, and hundreds of others.

Specialty Online Directories

Specialty directories limit the scope of their content to a specific topic area.

BUSINESS DIRECTORIES

You may want to check out directories that focus on business, including:

■ CEOExpress: *www.ceoexpress.com*

■ Brint.com: *www.brint.com*

YELLOW PAGES DIRECTORIES

Yellow pages directories can provide a quick way to locate the address or telephone number of a specific business.

- Yellowpages.com: *www.yellowpages.com*

- Switchboard: *www.switchboard.com*

- Yellow.com: *www.yellow.com*

- Google Local: *http://maps.google.com*

- Yahoo Yellow Pages: *http://yp.yahoo.com*

WHITE PAGES DIRECTORIES

White pages directories can help you find addresses and phone numbers for individuals whose information has been listed by telephone companies.

- 411.com: *www.411.com*

- Whitepages.com: *www.whitepages.com*

- Yahoo People Search: *http://people.yahoo.com*

The Wayback Machine

Want to find something that's disappeared from the Web? The Internet is an excellent source of information, but websites often disappear, seemingly lost forever. There is, however, a resource that preserves them. The Internet Archive is a nonprofit organization building a "library" of the Internet by continually collecting and storing billions of website pages. The Archive works with institutions such as the Library of Congress and the Smithsonian. Using what they call the "Wayback Machine," you can quickly view websites that have disappeared and older versions of current websites. Check it out at: *www.archive.org*.

CHAPTER 11

Business Research Databases

Many of the resources you'll explore when conducting business research will take the form of databases or websites that access information from databases. Broadly defined, a database is simply a collection of data—quantitative or qualitative—stored on one or more computers and arranged in a way that makes it easy for researchers to retrieve.

Business research databases can take many different forms, including:

- Websites

- CD-ROMs

- Software installed on a computer

Some, like the U.S. Census Bureau's websites, offer free access to everyone. Others can cost thousands of dollars and are generally licensed for use to institutions, agencies, or businesses and require a fee or special access privileges. These include library databases, available for use by members of the library community. Public library database access is free with a library card; college or university library databases are usually available without charge to students, faculty, and other members of the university community. Other researchers may be able to access these for a fee, if public access is permitted at all.

In general, business research databases are compiled by large companies, including Thomson Gale (which produces databases like InfoTrac) or Ovid Technologies (ABI/Inform Global), by governments, or by educational institutions. These organizations are able to employ a variety of programmers, knowledge management specialists, statisticians, researchers, writers, and editors to gather the information their databases contain, determine which of it to include, and decide how to best organize it for easy and efficient retrieval.

You can locate wide spectrum of information through databases. Some allow you to find and actually tabulate numerical data. Others retrieve information including:

- Journal articles

- Market research reports

- Names and addresses of businesses

- Executive profiles and contact information

- Mapped geographic locations

- Demographic data

- Psychographic data (lifestyles and interests)

■ Choosing a Database

The value of a database depends on how easily it helps you find the information you need and the quality of the information you find, as it relates to your project. So to some extent, a database's value is subjective and project-specific. However, there are some key characteristics to look for whenever you're choosing a database:

- **Easy to navigate.** Finding your way around the database is intuitive. You don't need any special skills or instructions to locate the information you're seeking.

- **Easy to search.** You can find the information you need in just a few steps and can use a variety of options—such as searching by keyword, author, title, NAICS code or zip code—to locate it.

- **Helpful search result format.** Your search results are organized in a logical and useful manner. Some databases provide abstracts that enable you to determine the extent to which the information you've uncovered is relevant to your topic.

- **Comprehensive.** The database contains a large body of information, ranging from reports and articles to statistical data.

- **Up-to-date.** The database features information compiled within at least the last three years. (This is less relevant when seeking historical information.)

- **Quality of data.** The database includes information from reputable sources that adhere to professional standards when gathering their data. For example, the database's market survey results reflect groups of respondents that are large and varied enough to represent the general population. News articles should come from well-known news sources or from smaller media outlets that use similar techniques and ethics in gathering information.

■ Some Top Databases

While you will find many excellent databases listed in this book, here are a few that satisfied most or all of the criteria above and retrieved useful data. (Note: Because this book already features a chapter on Government Resources on pages 71-78, the databases of the U.S. Census Bureau and other U.S. government agencies are not listed below. Be sure to acquaint yourself with these excellent resources, especially when seeking industry or target market data.)

Free Databases

BUSINESS & COMPANY RESOURCE CENTER

You'll find a wide range of easy-to-access information in this database, including industry overviews, company rankings, profiles, histories, brand information, investment reports, and more. This database can be accessed through public or college and university libraries. (For more on this resource, see pages 97 and 145.)

INFOTRAC

This popular database, usually available through public or college and university libraries, is particularly helpful in tracking down hard-to-find company and trade information. It categorizes millions of articles mainly from magazines and reference books, ranging from mainstream publications to more specialized sources. (For more on this resource, see page 152.)

REFERENCEUSA

If you want to zero in on company information for a particular region, such as an area code, this database is a great place to start. It covers more than twelve million businesses in the U.S. and one million in Canada and includes such information as companies in a particular area, revenue figures, and company backgrounds. You may even find names, addresses, phone numbers, and other information on key company executives. ReferenceUSA also serves as useful research tool for industry and target market data. It's available through public or college and university libraries. (For more on this resource, see page 156.)

Fee-Based Databases

ABI/INFORM GLOBAL

This database indexes and abstracts journal articles in the areas of business conditions, trends, management techniques, corporate strategies, and industry-specific topics worldwide. It's a good place to find articles on your industry and competition. The database covers 60,000 companies and features nearly 1,800 leading business and management periodicals, including respected journals such as *Journal of Business Ethics* and *Journal of the Academy of Marketing*. You can also retrieve full articles from the *Wall Street Journal*, the only newspaper on the database. (For more on this resource, see page 115.)

MINTEL

Use this excellent database for detailed target market information on consumer life-style and psychographic behavior as it relates to a wide range of industries, products and life stages. It also provides current data on industry trends and consumer buying habits. It's available through many university libraries. (For more on this resource, see pages 124 and 263.)

Research Firms

For accurate information about industries, corporations depend on private research firms that collect and analyze data. These firms typically specialize in a particular sector, such as technology or health care. Their research reports are highly regarded by corporate leaders, but typically, are very expensive unless your company—or college/university library—subscribes to their databases. If you don't have access through a university, check online to see if individual reports of interest are available for purchase.

Leading research firms in the technology sector include:

- Dataquest: *www.dataquest.com*

- eMarketer: *www.emarketer.com*

- Forrester: *www.forrester.com*

- The Gartner Group: *www.gartner.com*

- Jupiter Communications: *www.jupiterresearch.com*

A list of research firms can be found at Infotech Trends: *www.infotechtrends.com/free_research.htm*

NOTES:

CHAPTER 12

Government Resources

The United States government compiles an immense amount of statistical information, both about the people of the U.S. and about the American economy, including in-depth financial data on industries. State governments also compile data about economic activity in individual U.S. states. And, to a lesser degree, many county or city governments also gather local statistics. The Canadian government, likewise, compiles a huge amount of statistical data on the Canadian economy and population. You'll find this government-compiled data to be extremely useful. Moreover, it's free!

In addition to being affordable and easily accessible (with any Internet connection), government statistics have a number of advantages over other sources:

■ Government statistics are often compiled from actual numbers rather than being derived from samples. For instance, the U.S. Census Bureau's population numbers are based on counting virtually every U.S. resident. Thus, this data is likely to be more accurate than data derived from extrapolating from a small representative sample.

■ In most cases, government statistics are based on very large numbers, typically yielding more accurate results than data based on small samples.

■ The data tends to be conservative rather than speculative. Government sources are generally cautious in their approach to numbers. They are less likely to inflate numbers merely to make an industry or company seem healthier than it actually is.

■ The data can sometimes be compiled from sensitive sources (such as tax returns) that would otherwise be unavailable to researchers.

QUICK**TIP**

Shop Around

Many different government agencies collect and gather statistical data. Check a number of government websites for the information that's most relevant to your search.

◼ U.S. Government Data Portals

The U.S. government has created a few easy-to-use online entry points—or *portals*—to help researchers quickly find data gathered by government agencies. These portals are good first stops when looking for government-gathered information.

FIRSTGOV

www.firstgov.gov

Billed as "The U.S. Government's Official Web Portal," this site is designed to be the main gateway to all government information—not just statistical data. Since this site is designed to serve the public for all contact with the U.S. government, it can appear overwhelming.

For business research go to the home page and click on:

- the tab for Businesses and Nonprofits

  or

- the link to Data and Statistics in the left-hand column

FEDSTATS

www.fedstats.gov

If you want numbers, you'll find them here! This page is the main entry to statistics compiled by over one hundred federal agencies. You can search by topic, government agency, state, or by clicking on maps.

Particularly helpful easy-to-use links at FedStats include:

- Topic Links, A-Z

- MapStats

- Data Access Tools

- Statistics by Geography from U.S. Agencies

U.S. Census Bureau

www.census.gov

The U.S. Census Bureau offers a vast array of highly valuable data—for free. In particular, the Census Bureau provides comprehensive demographic information useful for target market research and compiles detailed reports on specific industries. Many private research companies rely to some extent on Census data.

If you explore the U.S. Census Bureau's website, you'll find a great deal of informative data. Moreover, the Bureau has made much of its data easily accessible through several user-friendly entry-points. These include:

AMERICAN FACTFINDER

www.factfinder.census.gov

An easy-to-use portal for finding Census Bureau data, whether on people or businesses. One quick and easy way to retrieve demographic data is to get a "Fact Sheet" on a geographic area by entering a city, county, zip code, or state name in the search box provided on the home page.

QUICKFACTS

http://quickfacts.census.gov

Another easy-to-use access point for summaries of the most-requested data for states and counties. Includes data such as population by age, ethnicity, education, and income levels. Once you have selected a state, city, or county, you can get links to more statistics for that area by clicking on **More data sets**.

COUNTY BUSINESS PATTERNS

www.census.gov/epcd/cbp/view/cbpview.html

This data source is a gem, especially if you are looking for economic patterns and business activity at a local, county, metropolitan area, or state level. For instance, you can find the number and size of drycleaners in a specific zip code or the number of dental labs in a county. Searching this site, especially viewing data using NAICS codes is fast and easy. (For more on NAICS codes, see pages 25-27.)

QUICK**TIP**

Firms and Establishments

Keep in mind that the U.S. Census Bureau distinguishes between *firms* and *establishments*:

- Firms are individual companies, regardless of how many locations they have. The McDonald's Corporation is one firm.

- Establishments are individual locations. McDonald's is composed of thousands of establishments across the U.S.

THE ECONOMIC CENSUS

www.census.gov/econ/census02/

Every five years, the U.S. government—through the Census Bureau—compiles an Economic Census of the U.S. The Economic Census produces in-depth reports on industries, organized by NAICS code (for more on NAICS codes, see pages 25-27). These lengthy reports provide highly detailed data, particularly for the U.S. as a whole. Statistics for local areas are often withheld to avoid disclosing information about individual firms.

AMERICAN COMMUNITY SURVEY

www.census.gov/acs/www/

The American Community Survey is a survey of three million households that the Census Department conducts every year. It is designed to provide detailed information on a wide variety of lifestyle and demographic topics, including income, commute times, home ownership, and more. You can also access this information through the American FactFinder site (see page 73).

STATISTICAL ABSTRACT OF THE U.S.

www.census.gov/statab/www/

Since 1878, the U.S. government has published an annual statistical overview of virtually every aspect of American society and economy. You'll find in-depth statistics on an amazingly broad array of topics. You can also find historical data going back to 1881.

▦ U.S. Bureau of Labor Statistics

www.bls.gov

The Bureau of Labor Statistics compiles data about the American economy relating to employment. This data encompasses a great variety of topics including employment rates, labor force profiles, the health of industries, wages, consumer spending, and much more. Check the A-Z Index in the upper right-hand corner of the home page to find specific information.

Key data websites from the Bureau of Labor Statistics include:

INDUSTRY AT A GLANCE

www.bls.gov/iag/iaghome.htm

Industry at a Glance consists of summaries of statistics from twelve major economic "supersectors," including construction, manufacturing, wholesale and retail trade, information, and professional and business services. This resource is particularly good for a quick overview of these large sectors of the economy.

OCCUPATIONAL OUTLOOK HANDBOOK

www.bls.gov/oco/home.htm

This handbook contains detailed descriptions of hundreds of different types of jobs, including statistics relating to employment, wages, future job growth prospects, and links to useful sites relating to those jobs. This resource is particularly good for finding growth projections for specific job categories or assessing average wages for those jobs. Use the A-Z Index on the home page to locate data on individual job categories.

CAREER GUIDE TO INDUSTRIES (CGI)

www.bls.gov/oco/cg/home.htm

This site provides general overviews of dozens of industries, including the average wages and type and number of jobs in those industries.

ECONOMY AT A GLANCE

www.bls.gov/eag/home.htm

Employment-related data available by state or metropolitan area. Easy to use.

■ U.S. Department of Commerce

BUREAU OF ECONOMIC ANALYSIS, DEPARTMENT OF COMMERCE

www.bea.gov

This site contains detailed economic data, including GDP (Gross Domestic Product) by industry or state, and personal income at state and local levels. It can be challenging to navigate.

ECONOMICS AND STATISTICS ADMINISTRATION, DEPARTMENT OF COMMERCE

www.esa.doc.gov

The ESA provides statistical information to government entities to assist in making policy. Its components include the U.S. Census Bureau, the Bureau of Economic Analysis, and Stat-USA (a fee-based statistical service of the U.S. government). At this site, search **Reports** or click on **Economic Indicators** on the home page.

ECONOMIC INDICATORS, DEPARTMENT OF COMMERCE

www.economicindicators.gov/

This site brings together the most recent economic statistical reports from the U.S. Census Bureau and the Bureau of Economic Analysis. It covers issues such as GDP (Gross Domestic Product), new construction, retail and wholesale trade, and personal income. It is best for very recent data.

■ Other U.S. Government Resources

EDGAR DATABASE/U.S. SECURITIES AND EXCHANGE COMMISSION

http://www.sec.gov/edgar.shtml

Every company traded publicly in the U.S. must file reports with the Securities and Exchange Commission, the agency responsible for overseeing the stock exchanges in the U.S. These reports include details of earnings and profitability and much more. EDGAR (Electronic Data Gathering Analysis and Retrieval) is the system for electronically accessing the data contained in these company filings.

U.S. PATENT AND TRADEMARK OFFICE

www.uspto.gov

The U.S. Patent and Trademark Office allows an easy online search of its database of registered patents and trademarks. This information can be especially helpful if you're developing a potentially competitive product or trying to find a name or slogan for your own company. Doing your homework here may help you avoid patent or trademark legal difficulties later.

INTERNAL REVENUE SERVICE

www.irs.ustreas.gov/taxstats/index.html

The agency responsible for collecting taxes has compiled detailed statistics derived from tax returns. In particular, the Corporation Source Book provides useful information on average income and expenses of companies by industry. To find the Corporation Source Book, click on **Corporations** under the heading **Business Tax Statistics** on the home page, then select **Corporate Source Book**.

NATIONAL BUREAU OF ECONOMIC RESEARCH

www.nber.org/

This is not a government site. However, this private, nonprofit, nonpartisan organization provides statistical evaluation on many national economic topics. Background reports offer valuable insight into critical economic issues. A feast for data junkies!

■ State and Local Government Resources

When seeking data on a particular location, one place to check for statistics and information is the website of the government of that specific area (city, county, or state). If, for instance, you are deciding whether to locate your business in one of two different cities, you may want to check with the city, county, and state government websites of those cities to gather economic data that might affect the future health of your company.

If you're looking for information about a private company, you can often find basic information (such as the owner's name, address, and date of incorporation) on companies that are incorporated in a state through the Secretary of State's office.

Other places to check when seeking information about a specific area include local:

- Small Business Development Centers

- Chambers of Commerce

- Better Business Bureaus

- College or university libraries or business departments

STATE DATA CENTERS

www.census.gov/sdc/www/

The U.S. Census Bureau maintains a network of data providers nationwide, including state offices, universities, and county and regional governments. Click on the state of interest on the home page and click on subsequent links to locate data providers for your state or area.

LIBRARY OF CONGRESS DIRECTORY OF STATE GOVERNMENTS

www.loc.gov/rr/news/stategov/stategov.html

The U.S. Library of Congress maintains this page linking to state government websites.

STATE AND LOCAL GOVERNMENT ON THE NET

www.statelocalgov.net

One of the easiest ways to locate state or local government information available online is through this privately operated website. Click on the state of interest to find links to state, county, and local websites.

SPERLING'S BEST PLACES

www.bestplaces.net

A very cool site. Privately operated by the research company that compiles statistical "Best Places" studies, this is a quick, easy, and fun way to get detailed data on a city.

■ Canadian Government Resources

STATISTICS CANADA

www.statcan.ca

This is the main entry point for locating government-compiled data on all aspects of Canadian life, including businesses and population. It is extremely easy to use. You can search by keyword. Or, after you have selected English as your language on the home page, click on:

- **Canadian Statistics** to locate data on a wide variety of aspects of the Canadian economy and population, including data by province or metropolitan area;

  or

- **Community Profiles** to go to an in-depth statistical analysis of a specific Canadian community.

CANADIAN ECONOMY ONLINE

www.canadianeconomy.gc.ca/english/economy/

This site provides easy access to a wide variety of recent statistics about the Canadian economy. In the left-hand column under **Learn About**, click **Economic Concepts** for a quick and easy-to-understand backgrounder on key aspects of any economy and how that concept affects Canada.

CHAPTER 13

Media Websites

Print publications and other media outlets are excellent resources for up-to-date information on a wide variety of business topics. You can usually access these outlets through their Internet sites.

In addition to their continually changing news stories, media websites often provide a number of research resources, such as backgrounders on industries and companies. Moreover, they typically maintain archives of their previously published articles—often going back many years. These archives can be outstanding sources of information, particularly overviews and histories of industries, companies, or products.

Since the articles on media websites are usually written for the general public, they're easily comprehensible, even for those not previously familiar with an industry.

Note: Many of the following sites charge small fees for archived articles.

■ Business/Financial Websites

These websites, focusing on business topics, were created especially for the Internet. Often aimed at investors, they generally include substantial background information on companies and industries. Typically, they also offer in-depth business news. These sites also occasionally offer archives of previously released material.

- Marketwatch from DowJones: *www.marketwatch.com*

- CNN Money: *http://money.cnn.com*

- Reuters: *www.reuters.com*

- Yahoo! Finance: *http://finance.yahoo.com*

- MSN Money: *www.moneycentral.msn.com*

- AllBusiness: *www.allbusiness.com*

■ Business/Financial Newspapers

You can access the archives of most business newspapers through their websites (in some cases for a small fee). These articles provide in-depth coverage of industries, people, companies, markets. Local business journals typically compile lists of leading local companies by industry. Generally, these papers tend to be relatively neutral, objective sources of information.

- Wall Street Journal: *www.wsj.com* (subscription required)

- American City Business Journals: *www.bizjournals.com*

- Financial Times: *www.ft.com*

- Investors Business Daily: *www.investors.com*

- Crain's local business newspapers: *www.crain.com*

■ Business and Finance Periodicals

Virtually all business magazines also maintain robust websites containing current information, research tools, and archives. They are a good source for in-depth articles on companies, individuals, and industries, as well as forecasts and analysis. Some publications compile rankings of companies or individuals (for example, the Fortune 500 Top Companies, Forbes' 400 Richest Americans, and INC's 100 fastest-growing companies) that are included on their websites.

- BusinessWeek: *www.businessweek.com*

- Fortune: *www.fortune.com*

- Business 2.0: *www.business2.com*

- Forbes: *www.forbes.com*

- Inc.: *www.inc.com*

- The Economist: *www.economist.com*

- Red Herring: *www.redherring.com*

◼ Industry and Trade Periodicals

Virtually every industry has one magazine or journal (or more) covering news relating to that industry. Many of these periodicals are published by the trade association serving that industry. Others, especially those serving larger industries, are published by media companies.

Industry publications provide in-depth articles and data about companies, individuals, and trends in an industry. They can also provide valuable historical perspectives on the industry as a whole. Check their advertisements to learn about vendors and suppliers to that industry.

To locate trade and industry periodicals visit:

- ◼ Internet Public Library list of magazines: *www.ipl.org/div/serials/*

- ◼ University of Florida list of industry journals: *web.uflib.ufl.edu/cm/business/journals/ tradejournals.htm*

- ◼ Open Directory Project list of industry news sources: *http://dmoz.org/Business/ News_and_Media/By_Industry/*

- ◼ The Planning Shop's list of industry associations: *www.planningshop.com/ associations*

◼ Local and General Interest Newspapers

Virtually all general interest newspapers serving mid- to large-sized communities maintain websites. These sites typically provide access to articles from past issues, often going back many years. Local newspapers are a good source of background information about a target market and of historical information and news about a company located in that community. Be aware that newspapers typically report on research conducted by others rather than being the source of original data.

NewsLibrary.com allows you to search hundreds of news sources or identify news sources in the community that interests you. Other sites to explore include:

- ◼ NewsLibrary.com: *www.newslibrary.com*

- ◼ Library of Congress list of news resources on the Web: *www.loc.gov/rr/news/lists.html*

- ◼ Internet Public Library list of newspapers worldwide: *www.ipl.org/div/news/*

- ◼ USA Today Money: *www.usatoday.com/money*

- ◼ New York Times: *www.nytimes.com*

Brokerage Analyst Reports

Stock brokerage firms and other financial investment companies assign analysts to track the performance of both individual companies and entire industries in order to assist their clients in making investment decisions. These analysts monitor the trade press and general news reports, analyze financial documents and stock performance, and often participate in phone calls with company executives.

Since publicly traded companies are required to make certain financial (and other) information public, and analysts follow and accumulate data from a variety of sources, studying their reports can be an excellent means of gathering information about a company or industry.

Analysts not only develop an overview of the industry or company and evaluate its financial performance, they typically also offer opinions on the future prospects for that specific company or industry.

Because these reports are designed to guide investors—primarily those with an interest in the stock market—analyst reports tend to focus on:

- Publicly traded companies
- Larger industries (likely to be dominated by publicly traded companies)

The types of information you can get from analyst reports include:

- Stock performance
- Financial data, including sales and profits
- Market share data
- Product line sales
- Recent activities
- Announcements of future plans
- Compensation of executives

Access

If you have an account with a stock brokerage company or work with a financial advisor, you may have access to reports from that company. Check their websites or ask your broker or other financial advisor.

Some analyst reports are available free through business databases at your public library. A good one to try is the Business and Company Resource Center database (see pages 97 and 145). After you select a company, click on Investment Reports.

If you are a college or university student, the databases available at your business library databases will provide access to many analyst reports.

Part IV: Straight to the Numbers You Need

CHAPTER 14

Straight to the Numbers

In the chapters that follow, you'll learn how to find the business information you need—fast!

Rather than simply providing you with a list of places to look for information, the chapters in this section show you exactly how to navigate some of the business databases and websites you're likely to use when conducting business research. Working your way through these databases and websites on your own can be confusing, so the following pages show you how a research project could be conducted—step-by-step.

The resources described here are among the most useful for conducting business research. They are categorized into three of the most important areas of business research—areas that are vital for developing a business plan or other key strategic business documents:

■ Industry

■ Company

■ Target Market

To illustrate how to conduct an effective search using these resources, many sample searches are included. In general, the sample searches illustrate the process of locating the kinds of information a (fictional) computer training company in Indianapolis, Indiana, might be looking for when developing a business plan. When no information about the computer training industry was available, the samples show searches for information relating to the publishing industry.

As you conduct your own research, it will be useful to remember how certain terms are used—especially by key sources such as the U.S. Census Bureau. See page 6 for definitions of these terms.

Reviewing the sample searches on the pages ahead will make it easier for you to conduct your own business research, on both the sites and databases shown here and on other business research resources. Keep in mind, however, that the look of websites and databases can change. The designs you see on the following screen shots could have changed—in either minor or major ways—by the time you visit a particular site.

■ Resources versus Sources

Throughout this book, the terms *resources* and *sources* are used to mean:

■ **Resources:** Databases or websites that compile and organize information and/or data from multiple outlets; frequently, the information or data found there is created or collected by others—the original sources of the information.

■ **Sources:** Research organizations or other creators or collectors of information or data; the originators of such information. This information is often compiled along with information from other original sources by research resources.

As you conduct your business research and collect information, make absolutely certain that you note both the original source of the data and the resource where you located it (if they are different). You will need to cite these sources and resources, especially in business plans and academic papers. Investors and others may question you about your data, and you'll have more credibility if you can cite its source. Moreover, you'll likely return to the source for future research or to double check your data.

For information on how to appropriately cite your research sources, see pages 53-55.

■ Free and Fee-based Resources

The business research resources featured in the chapters that follow are classified as *free* or *fee-based*:

■ **Free resources** include databases and websites that are available to you either without charge on the Internet or from many, if not most, public libraries.

■ **Fee-based resources** include databases and websites that require either a subscription fee or payment on a per-use basis. Such charges can range from ten to many thousands of dollars. Most of the fee-based resources listed on the following pages are likely to be subscribed to by college or university libraries, and, thus, are available without charge to those who have access to those libraries.

■ Access

To gain access to any of the resources listed in this book, you'll need a public or academic library card and, in some instances, a credit card:

■ **Public library card.** Most public libraries, especially in larger communities, maintain subscriptions to databases of business information. If you have a card from the public library whose databases you want to access, you can typically access them either from a computer inside the library or an Internet connection outside the library. If you are using your public library's resources from outside the library (online), you may need to unblock your Internet security programs to access some databases.

■ **College/university library card.** College and university libraries, especially larger university and business libraries, maintain subscriptions to business and research databases. Using your library card number, you can access these databases either from a computer inside the library or an Internet connection outside the library. Many university libraries also allow limited access to members of the public without campus library cards (often for a small fee), although not all databases may be available to them.

■ **Credit card.** The information from many fee-based resources, especially data from private research companies, is available to corporations and the general public—for a price. Often, the information available for purchase may be somewhat more recent than the data available through university libraries. However, this data can be expensive to buy; prices range from ten to many thousands of dollars.

Use the resources and samples on the pages that follow to learn research techniques you can apply to any resource and to guide you straight to the numbers you need for your current research project.

CHAPTER 15

Researching an Industry

Imagine you're starting a new business. You've got a great idea, you've brought together a solid management team, you've even raised the start-up money. There's only one problem: your industry is in trouble.

You don't build a business in a vacuum. Trends affecting your industry affect your business, too. Knowing what's going on in your industry enables you to better compete and succeed.

If you are seeking financing for your business, potential funders will certainly ask about existing industry conditions and trends. You'll make a more positive impression—and have a better chance of getting funded—if you have industry data that supports your business plan.

In addition to educating yourself about your specific industry, it's a good idea to look at the health of the broad economic sector to which your industry belongs (for example, manufacturing, retail, transportation, or services). Past performance in, and growth projections for, this broad economic sector give you a sense of the economic environment in which your industry operates. If you're thinking of opening a bookstore, it's useful to see what's happening in the entire retail sector.

However, while examining broad economic sectors can provide useful insights into business conditions, the most important data you can collect concerns your specific industry. After all, even if the retail sector as a whole is thriving, bookstores may face unique pressures.

Finding industry data helps you:

- Understand conditions and trends your business may encounter, so you'll be better prepared to deal with them.
- Gather solid facts and figures to help you prepare a more realistic business plan and build a better company.
- Demonstrate to potential financing sources (investors and lenders) that you have a good grasp of external business conditions and a realistic plan for your business.

Tips for Finding Industry Information

1. Begin with an industry overview. Read a few articles that give you a sense of the history of and trends in an industry. It's tempting to go straight to the numbers—to find statistical data first—but a general overview will give you insights that can help shape your research process and define industry terms you may be unfamiliar with. Good sources for general overviews of an industry include:

   ■ General business media websites and publications

   ■ Industry-specific publications

   ■ Analyst reports

2. Find the NAICS code for your industry. Knowing the numerical code that identifies your specific industry makes it much easier to find information, especially statistical data. For information on how to find your NAICS code, see pages 25-27.

3. Make a list of terms that can be used to describe your industry or key aspects of the industry. Most industries can be identified in more than one way. A dairy, for instance, can also be called a *milk producer* or be referred to as *cattle farming*. Having a variety of different terms to describe your industry at your fingertips will help when you're conducting keyword searches.

4. Check out your industry's trade association. Trade associations are good places to find statistical data, projections of industry trends, and links to other sources of information. A list of many trade association websites is available at: *www.planningshop.com/associations*.

   When you're exploring a trade association website, look for tabs/topics such as:

   ■ Press/media/news

   ■ Research

   ■ About the industry

   ■ Industry publications

5. Make a list of key statistics and information about the industry you are researching. Look over the list of suggested industry topics that follows and fill out the worksheet on pages 94-95 to better define the focus of your industry research.

■ Types of Industry Information to Research

When searching for information about an industry, focus on such issues as:

■ **A general industry overview and analysis**

■ **Current and historical financial performance of the industry, including:**
- Total revenues, overall and by product lines, if possible
- Total number of units sold, by product lines, if possible
- Total profits and/;or average profit margins
- Growth rates over the past few years

■ **Companies in the industry, including:**
- Total number of companies
- Leading companies in the industry
- Total employment in the industry
- Market share distribution of each company

■ **The industry's performance in relation to your target market (geographic and demographic), including:**
- Total revenues and profits from that target market
- Number of companies serving that target market and market leaders
- Trends relating to that target market

■ **Impact of seasonal changes and/or economic cycles on the industry**

■ **Trends and forecasts, especially projected future growth rate of the industry**

■ **Industry resources, including major suppliers/vendors, trade publications, associations, and research companies**

■ WORKSHEET: Industry Research

Use this worksheet to record key information about the industry you are researching.

■ **A general industry overview and analysis**

_____

_____

_____

_____

_____

_____

_____

_____

_____

_____

_____

_____

_____

_____

_____

_____

_____

_____

_____

_____

_____

_____

_____

_____

_____

_____

■ **Current and historic financial performance of the industry, including:**

• Total revenues, overall and by product lines, if possible

_____

• Total number of units sold, by product lines, if possible

_____

• Total profits and/or average profit margins

_____

• Growth rates over the past few years

_____

■ **Companies in the industry, including:**

• Total number of companies

_____

• Leading companies in the industry

_____

• Total employment in the industry

_____

• Market share distribution of each company

_____

■ **The industry's performance in relation to your target market (geographic and demographic), including:**

• Total revenues and profits from that target market

_____

• Number of companies serving that target market and market leaders

_____

• Trends relating to that target market

_____

_____

■ Impact of seasonal changes and/or economic cycles on the industry

_____

_____

■ Trends and forecasts, especially projected future growth rate of the industry

_____

_____

■ Industry resources, including major suppliers/vendors, trade publications, associations, and research companies

_____

_____

NOTES:

_____

_____

_____

_____

_____

_____

_____

_____

_____

_____

_____

_____

_____

RESEARCHING AN INDUSTRY

FREE RESOURCES

▪ Business & Company Resource Center

Access at: Public or college/university libraries.

Overview: This resource compiles many different forms of business data, including industry overviews, company rankings, profiles, histories, brand information, investment reports, and more. (A comprehensive list of the periodicals featured in this database is available at *www.galegroup.com/tlist/sb5114.html*.) For more on this resource and another sample search, see page 145.

Best for: Finding industry news and overviews.

SAMPLE SEARCH

The goal of this search is to locate an overview of the book publishing industry around the world.

From your library's home page, navigate to **Business & Company Resource Center**. It's usually included in the References/Database section of the library's site. If you have difficulty locating it, ask your librarian for assistance.

1. When you have reached the **Business & Company Resource Center**, click on **Industry**.

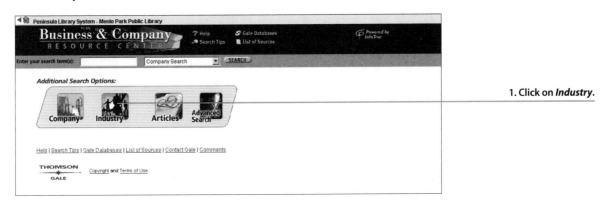

1. Click on *Industry*.

2. In the second search field on the **Industry** page, next to **Enter Industry Description**, enter *publishing*. (*Note:* When entering keywords in the **Industry Description** field, be sure to choose a general industry category. You will have an opportunity to narrow it down on later pages.)

Alternatively, you can search by NAICS codes. (See pages 25-27 for more information on NAICS codes and where to find them.)

3. Click the **Search Description** button under the second search field.

2. Enter a general
description of your industry.

3. Click *Search Description*.

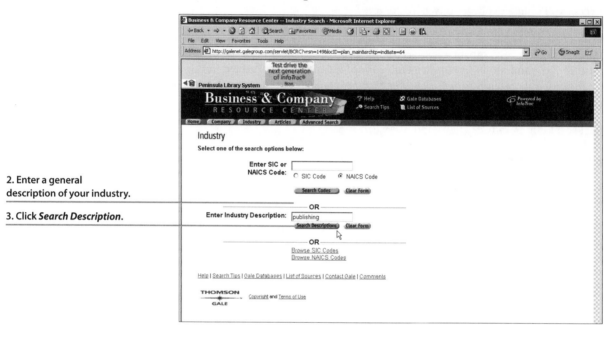

The search results page appears with a list of industry subsectors.

4. From the list, select **Books – Publishing, or Publishing and Printing**.

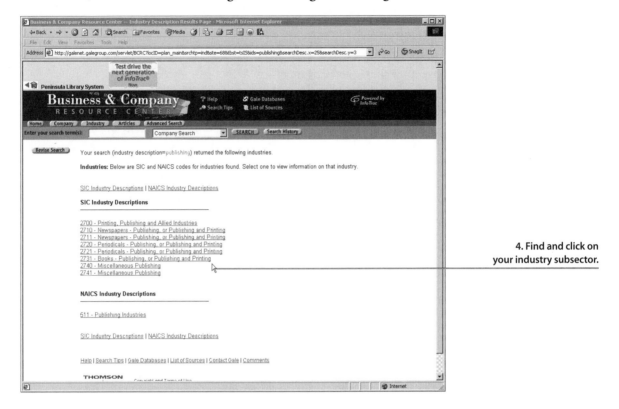

4. Find and click on
your industry subsector.

The search retrieves two encyclopedia entries on book publishing. (They appear to be the same document.)

5. Click the first entry.

5. Click the title to see if it provides useful information.

Result: The encyclopedia report provides a good overview of the international book publishing industry, including names, numbers, and insights into the industry's current status.

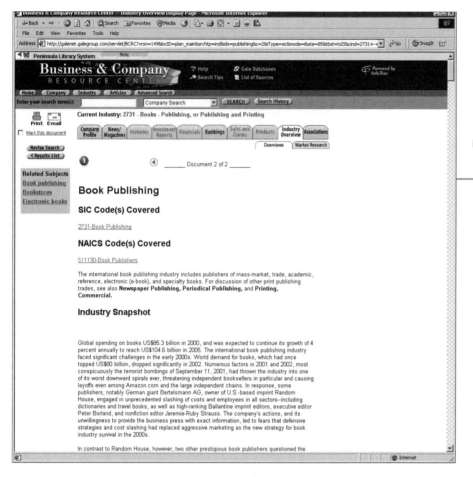

Result: An industry overview including book publishing industry descriptions, historical information, numerical data, and company names.

▨ RDS TableBase

Access at: Public or college/university libraries.

Overview: This international database presents numerical data (in table or chart format) on more than ninety industries worldwide. If you're looking for numbers, this is a good place to start. In addition to industry data, this resource provides product forecasts, company and brand rankings, information on market shares, and more. (*Note:* **TableBase** can vary in coverage—some areas are covered extensively; others only minimally.)

Best for: Finding numerical industry data.

SAMPLE SEARCH

This search will use **RDS TableBase** to discover how much the U.S. book publishing industry grossed in 2004.

From your local library's home page, navigate to **RDS TableBase**. It's usually included in the References/Database section of the library's home page. If you have difficulty locating it, ask your librarian for assistance.

1. When you arrive at the **RDS Reference Suite** home page, use the checkboxes to select **TableBase**.

2. Click **Start**.

1. Check the box for *TableBase*.

2. Click *Start*.

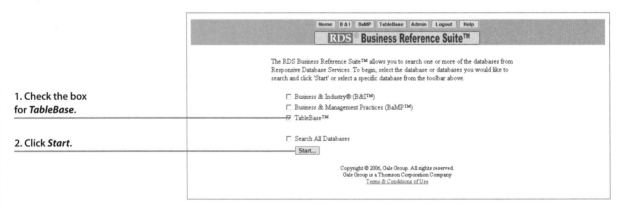

3. On the search form that appears, enter *Book publishing* in the search field.

4. Use the pull-down menus to select the most general search criteria (designated by the word **Any**). This will allow for the broadest search. (*Note:* Placing too many limits on a search can decrease its effectiveness.)

5. Click **Search** at the bottom of the page.

3. Enter *Book publishing* in the search field.

4. Select *Any* from all menus but Industry to allow for a broad search.

5. Click *Search*.

6. Scroll down to review the **TableBase** search results.

7. Select the article offering the most recent data.

8. Click the **Display Marked Articles** button at the bottom of the page.

6. Scroll down to review the results.

7. Use the checkbox to select the most recent book publishing industry data.

8. Click *Display Marked Articles*.

| Home | B & I | BaMP | TableBase | Admin | Logout | Help |

RDS® TableBase™

Search results, matches 1 - 19 of 19

Geographic Area:	United States
Words and Phrases:	Book Publishing
Industry:	Publishing

To view an article, click on the page icon 📄 next to the title. To mark an article for later retrieval, select the checkbox ☑ next to the title.

| Previous Page | Next Page | New Search | Refine Search |

Clear Marked Articles
Display Marked Articles

	Date	Title	Source	Text Available
1.	October 17, 2005	☐ 📄 Canada, Australia, New Zealand, United States, and United Kingdom English-language book publishing in production percentages for 2004	Publishers Weekly	☐ 📄
2.	May 30, 2005	☑ 📄 United States book publishing industry in number of new books produced and revenue in dollars for 1999 to 2004	Publishers Weekly	☐ 📄
3.	January 17, 2005	☐ 📄 United States Spanish-language book publishing market in number of copies sold for 200 to 2004	Publishers Weekly	☐ 📄
4.	April 05, 2004	☐ 📄 United States book publishing industry sales, both trade and total, in dollars for 1997 to 2003	Publishers Weekly	☐ 📄
5.	May 2003	☐ 📄 US market size for book publishing by sales in dollars, with annual percent change for each of nine book categories in 2001 and 2002	Graphic Arts Monthly	☐ 📄
6.	October 07, 2002	☐ 📄 US book publishing market size expressed as revenues in dollars by source for 2000 vs 1999, with purchased printing expenses and year-end inventories	Publishers Weekly	☐ 📄
7.	September 02, 2002	☐ 📄 US, Canada and the UK operating revenues and income in US dollars, Canadian dollars or pounds sterling for each of 14 publicly held book publishing companies in 2000 and 2001	Publishers Weekly	☐ 📄
8.	January 2002	☐ 📄 US book publishing market size expressed as net sales by category in dollars for 2001	Plunkett's Entertainment & Media Industry Almanac	☐ 📄
9.	January 2002	☐ 📄 US ranked profit or loss in dollars for each of 14 book publishing companies in 2000	Plunkett's Entertainment & Media Industry Almanac	☐ 📄
10.	August 20, 2001	☐ 📄 US top 50 media companies ranked by media-related revenues in dollars for 2000 vs 1999, with revenue breakdown for each of five media venues	Advertising Age	☐ 📄
11.	August 20, 2001	☐ 📄 US top 51 to 100 media companies ranked by media-related revenues in dollars for 2000 vs 1999, with revenue breakdown for each of five media venues	Advertising Age	☐ 📄
12.	February 26, 2001	☐ 📄 US book publishing industry market size as revenues in dollars for 1998 and 1999, with revenue breakdown from printed, multimedia, online and audio book sales, publication rights, contract printing and other revenues, expenses, and inventories	Publishers Weekly	☐ 📄
13.	August 28, 2000	☐ 📄 US book publishing market size expressed as sales in units and dollars by 12 industry segments for 1999 and forecast for 2000	Publishers Weekly	☐ 📄
14.	February 21, 2000	☐ 📄 US market size for book publishing as sales in dollars for 1998 and 1999, with sales breakdown for each of 18 market segments or sales venues	Publishers Weekly	☐ 📄
15.	January 01, 2000	☐ 📄 US top 18 media segments by percentage of total entertainment marketing programs for 1999	Entertainment Marketing Letter	☐ 📄
16.	September 28, 1998	☐ 📄 US advertising expenditures in dollars by News Corp for each of 13 types of media and for its top three brand names in 1997 vs 1996, with global sales and earnings, US and division sales, and operating income forecast for 1998 vs 1997	Advertising Age	☐ 📄
17.	December 01, 1997	☐ 📄 US book publishing industry sales in dollars via book clubs in 1985 to 1995	Direct Marketing Association (US) - Direct Marketing Statistics	☐ 📄
18.	December 01, 1997	☐ 📄 US book publishing industry sales in dollars via mail order publications in 1985 to 1995	Direct Marketing Association (US) - Direct Marketing Statistics	☐ 📄
19.	July 28, 1997	☐ 📄 Advertising spending, in dollars, on and by various types of media within the US communications industry for 1996 and 2001 forecast	Advertising Age	☐ 📄

| Previous Page | Next Page | New Search | Refine Search |

Clear Marked Articles
Display Marked Articles

Result: The most recent revenue figures for the book publishing industry, showing how many books were produced in the U.S. and the total amount spent on them in 2004.

| Home | B & I | BaMP | TableBase | Admin | Logout | Help |

RDS® TableBase™

| Send E-Mail | No Highlighting | | New Search |

How Do I Print/Save/Email Articles?

United States book publishing industry in number of new books produced and revenue in dollars for 1999 to 2

☑ 133636803
Title: Cranking it out.
Source: Publishers Weekly, 252 (22): 6, May 30, 2005. ISSN: 0000-0019
Publisher: Reed Business Information
Document Type: Journal
Record Type: Fulltext **Word Count:** 193
Publication Country: United States, **Language:** English
Table:

```
        Cranking It Out

                 1999      2000     2001      2002      2003      2004

New books
produced       119,000   122,000  141,000   147,000   121,000   195,000
Revenue in
billions        $23.9     $24.7    $24.7     $25.2     $25.9     $26.4

Note: Table made from line graph.

SOURCE: BOWKER, BISG
```

Copyright 2005 Reed Elsevier Inc.

Concept Terms: All market information; Output; Sales
Geographic Area: United States (USA); North America (NOAX)
Industry Names: Information industry; Publishing
Product Names: Books - publishing, or publishing and printing (273100)
Special Features: Table

Result: Total revenue produced by U.S. book publishers in 2004.

■ U.S. Census Bureau: American FactFinder Quick Reports

Access at: *http://factfinder.census.gov* or through the main page for the U.S. Census Bureau (*www.census.gov*). Select **American FactFinder** from the left-hand menu bar.

Overview: This section of the Census Bureau's site provides a quick reference for information on census-surveyed industries in an easily digestible format. You can search for the number of establishments, amount of sales, payroll, number of employees, and other statistics on a national, state, county, city, or zip code level. Each industry page also includes links to more detailed data.

Best for: Getting a quick snapshot of a census-surveyed national industry.

SAMPLE SEARCH

This search will locate an overview of the U.S. computer training industry with information on key states.

1. Select **Quick Reports** from the lower right-hand corner of the **FactFinder** home page.

1. Select *Quick Reports*

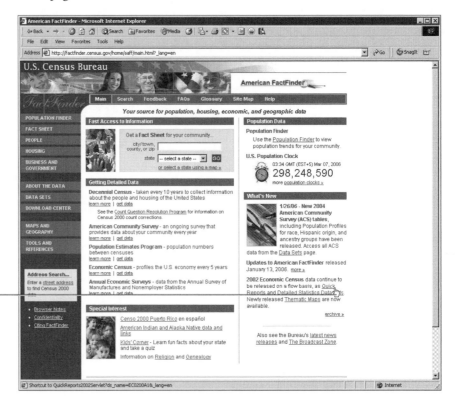

2. On the Quick Reports page, under **Industry Quick Reports**, click **the United States and states**.

2. Click to find national and state reports.

3. On the Select Industry page, enter the NAICS code for the computer training industry. (See pages 25-27 for more information on NAICS codes and how to find them.)

4. Click **Search**.

3. Enter the industry's NAICS code.

4. Click *Search*.

Provides a listing of NAICS codes for each industry.

5. The page refreshes and presents a scroll-down menu with the industries listed under the NAICS code you entered. Select the appropriate industry from the menu.

6. Click **Show Result**.

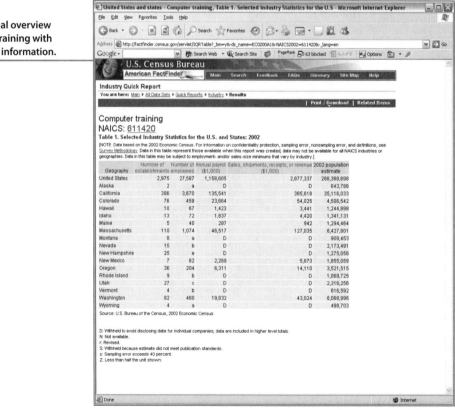

5. Select the appropriate industry.

6. Click *Show Result*.

Result: An overview of the computer training industry in the U.S. and in states with high concentrations of establishments in the industry.

Result: National overview of computer training with relevant state information.

◼ U.S. Census Bureau, Economic Census: Industry Series Reports

Access at: *www.census.gov/econ/census02/guide/INDSUMM.HTM* or through the U.S. Census Bureau home page (*www.census.gov*; in the **Business section**, click **Economic Series**).

Overview: These reports provide snapshots of twenty national industry sectors and hundreds of subsectors and industry groups. The data can be used for a variety of purposes: businesses can zero in on new markets, get a sense of an industry's profitability, or compare their own production and sales performance to that of the industry as a whole. You'll learn the number of establishments in the country, how much money they made, how much (in total) they paid their employees, what kinds of products they produced (if applicable), and how much they earned from each product line.

Best for: Researching the locations, strengths, and other characteristics of a national industry.

SAMPLE SEARCH

This search will locate data on the total number of computer training companies in the U.S. and their total revenue, based on the most recent census figures.

1. On the **Industry Series** home page, scan the categories and find **Educational Services**.

2. Click **More** to the left of the Educational Services category to retrieve the page.

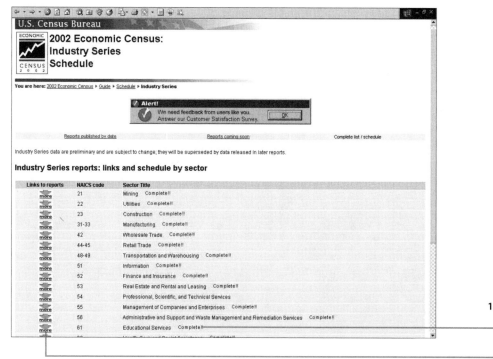

1. Find the *Educational Services* category.

2. Click *More*.

The category page appears and gives you the option of selecting the full report (with summaries of the data) or a report with tables only.

3. Click the **PDF** link under the **Full Report** column. This will retrieve a PDF version of the report.

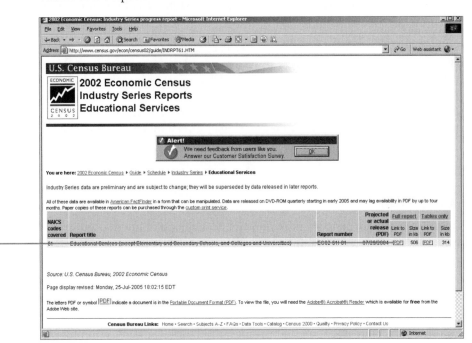

3. Select the *PDF* document for the full report.

4. Scroll down to read the full PDF report or use the icons in the upper left-hand corner of your window to print or save the document to your hard drive. Information on the number of computer training firms and their total revenue is highlighted on the screen image at the bottom of the page.

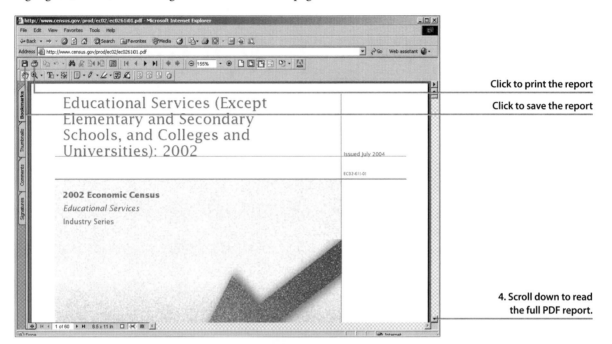

Result: The report shows the total number of computer training establishments in the U.S. and their total revenue in 2002.

RESEARCHING AN INDUSTRY

ADDITIONAL FREE RESOURCES

■ Industry Trade Associations

Access at: Each association's website; as well, BusinessFinance.com provides a great starting point for finding trade associations: *www.businessfinance.com/trade-associations.htm*. Another excellent resource for locating trade associations can be found at: *www.planningshop.com/associations*.

Overview: Trade associations offer a wealth of industry resources ranging from books, white papers, and PowerPoint presentations to industry experts who can provide insights and data for original research. The best resources are often available only to association members (who usually pay a fee to join the association), but with careful searching, you can find some excellent free resources as well.

Best for: Finding an insider's view of an industry.

■ Missouri Small Business Development Centers' Industry-Specific Guides

Access at: *www.missouribusiness.net/iag/index.asp*

Overview: These reports, compiled by the University of Missouri SBDC, profile more than fifty industries largely populated by small businesses. While their primary focus is Missouri businesses, the data may also be useful to those seeking industry information for other states. The reports for each industry include information on legal structure, taxes, hiring employees, and other issues, and provide links to additional reports.

Best for: Finding operational information for companies within an industry.

■ Rensselaer at Hartford University: Cole Library Industry Research Guides

Access at: *http://www.rh.edu/library/research.htm*

Overview: This Rensselaer University site serves as a convenient directory for industry-specific resources, including industry profiles, codes, financials and statistics, forecasts, and trade associations. Most of the resource listings feature short descriptions and links to additional information.

Best for: Finding a great starting point for a variety of information on an industry.

▣ U.S. Bureau of Labor Statistics: Career Guide to Industries (CGI)

Access at: *www.bls.gov/oco/cg/home.htm*

Overview: This federal government site is particularly helpful if you're interested in the job market from an industry's (rather than a job-seeker's) perspective. It covers dozens of industries, ranging from advertising to wholesale trade, and includes detailed information on employment practices, training, earnings, future job prospects, working conditions, and more. The guide offers plenty of facts and statistics about each industry, encompassing both a national and a state-by-state perspective. You can search for a specific industry using a search box or through the site's A-to-Z index.

Best for: Finding career or employment-related information on an industry.

▣ U.S. Bureau of Labor Statistics: Industry at a Glance

Access at: *www.bls.gov/iag/iaghome.htm*

Overview: The Census Bureau's **Industry-at-a-Glance** site provides labor-related information on twelve sectors: Construction, Education and Health Services, Financial Activities, Government, Information, Leisure and Hospitality, Manufacturing, Natural Resources and Mining, Other Services, Professional and Business Services, Transportation and Utilities, and Wholesale and Retail Trade. You'll find a variety of facts and statistics here, including number of workers employed by each sector, wage levels, labor productivity, labor costs, and layoff statistics.

Best for: Finding labor-related numerical data for an industry.

▣ ValuationResources.com: Industry Information Resources

Access at: *www.valuationresources.com/IndustryReport.htm*

Overview: Designed for business appraisers, business owners, and others interested in the value of industry investments, this free portal-type site provides links to a variety of industry resources. These include trade associations, publications, research firms, and other reputable sources of data. The site covers more than 350 industries, offering links to data on industry issues, trends, financial ratios, compensation, and many other valuation areas.

Best for: Finding investment-related industry information and resources.

Part IV: STRAIGHT TO THE NUMBERS YOU NEED

NOTES:

RESEARCHING AN INDUSTRY

FEE-BASED RESOURCES

ABI/INFORM Global (from ProQuest)

Access at: College/university libraries.

Overview: This database indexes and abstracts journal articles in the areas of business conditions, trends, management techniques, corporate strategies, and industry-specific topics worldwide. The resource features information on 60,000 companies and covers nearly 1,800 leading business and management periodicals, including respected journals such as *Journal of Business Ethics* and *Journal of the Academy of Marketing*. You can also retrieve full articles from the *Wall Street Journal*, the only newspaper on the database.

Best for: Finding articles about your industry and competition from hard-to-find trade publications, business journals, and the *Wall Street Journal*.

SAMPLE SEARCH

The site offers a variety of search options. This topic search for industry trade publications on computer training demonstrates one of the most efficient ways to find information.

1. Click **Topic** (or **Topic Guide**) at the top of the home page.

**1. Click *Topic Guide*
to search by topic.**

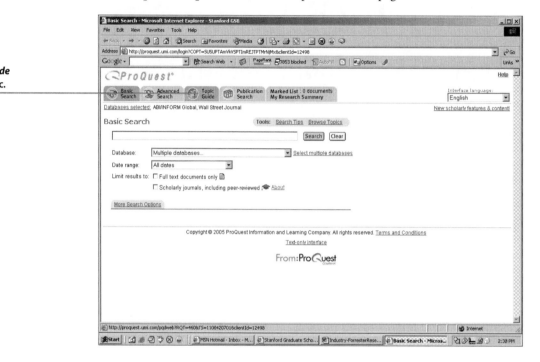

2. In the **Topic Guide** window, enter your search phrase in the search box—in this case, *computer training*.

3. Click **Find Term**.

2. Enter your search term in the field.

3. Click *Find Term*.

This retrieves a page with a list of relevant topics.

4. Click **View**.

4. Click *View* to see relevant articles.

If topic is too broad, clicking *Narrow* lets you add keywords to the search field.

The resulting page shows a list of articles related to your topic. You can narrow your results further by selecting a subtopic, date, or publication from the options box at the top of the page. You can also narrow results by selecting a specific type of publication from the tabs just above the article list.

5. Click the **Trade Publications** tab.

Box shows options for narrowing results by Topic, Date, or Publication.

5. Click tab to narrow results to *Trade Publications*.

Clicking **Trade Publications** narrows the list to articles from only those publications. You can sort the articles by most recent or most relevant. You can opt to view the listing, the full text of the article, an abstract summarizing its main points, or a PDF image of the journal pages featuring the article.

6. Click the article's title for listing information.

6. Click for additional information on the article.

Retrieves the full article.

Retrieves a PDF of the journal article pages.

Retrieves an abstract summarizing the main points.

The document information page features more information about the article, including the topics, companies, and locations it covers, its author, the publication in which it appeared, and its various database classifications.

7. Click **More Like This** just below the article listing to see similar articles.

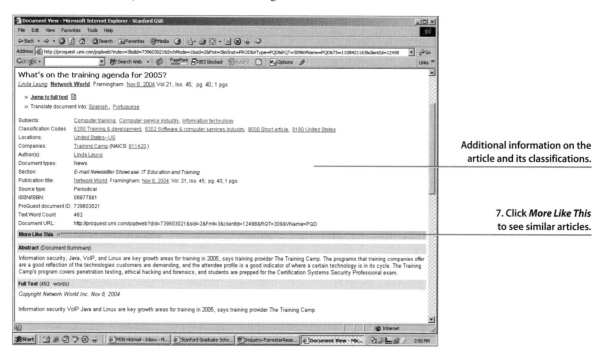

Additional information on the article and its classifications.

7. Click *More Like This* to see similar articles.

8. On the page that appears, use the check boxes to select the most relevant criteria.

8. Use check boxes to select criteria for additional articles.

Result: Several relevant trade articles to use for industry research.

Result: Three articles related to the topic.

■ Mintel

Access at: *http://www.mintel.com* (for fee-based reports) or college/university libraries. If accessing from a library, take a few minutes to create an account so you can store the reports you retrieve or create.

Overview: This excellent resource provides detailed, up-to-date information on industry trends and consumer behavior as they relate to a variety of business sectors, product decisions, life stages, and many other parameters. For more on this resource and another sample search, see page 263.

Best for: Analyzing an industry from many different angles, from market trends to consumer perceptions.

SAMPLE SEARCH

After you create an account and sign in, you can begin searching for relevant reports. There are several ways to search on this site. This sample search, for book industry market and trends data, uses one of the most direct methods.

1. Enter the appropriate keywords in the **Search Reports** field on the **Mintel Reports** home page (in this case, *book publishing*).

2. Click **Go**.

1. Enter industry keywords in the search reports field.

2. Click *Go*.

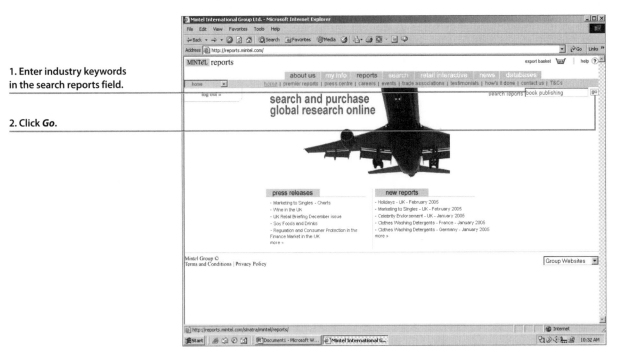

3. From the list on the search results page, choose a report likely to provide information relevant to your search and click the title. (**Book Retailing** has been selected here.)

3. Click the title to retrieve details on the report.

The next page outlines the various sections of the report. It also features news updates relevant to the report's topic on the right-hand side of the page.

4. Click the title of the section likely to retrieve the relevant information. (**Market Size & Trends** has been chosen here.) Use the checkboxes to make multiple selections.

Industry news updates.

4. Click the appropriate report section title.

Result: A page with the **Market Size & Trends** section of the report, which provides a host of important data on the U.S. retail book market. It includes a trend summary, total dollar sales, and percentage change in sales over the past six years.

Result: Market trend summary.

Total dollar sales.

Percentage change in sales.

■ Plunkett Research Online

Access at: College/university libraries.

Overview: This comprehensive resource provides data and information on a range of industry sectors and on many specific industries within each sector. The information is contained within its Industry Research Centers, which encompass thirty major industry sectors and many specific industries within each sector. For example, the Entertainment & Media Research Center contains information on such industries as newspapers, radio, television, and book publishing. Information includes market research and trends, company profiles, statistics, and industry associations.

Best for: Finding detailed financial data and forecasts on industry trends.

SAMPLE SEARCH

The Industry Research Center list provides the best starting point for using this site. It is also possible to use the search feature, but since the database is very large, this can be a much slower and more cumbersome process.

Here is a sample search for data on market trends affecting the computer training industry, starting at the Plunkett home page.

1. Scroll down the page to review the Industry Research Center list.

2. Find the most appropriate Research Center for your industry.

1. Scroll down to review the Industry Research Center list.

2. Find the appropriate industry sector from the list.

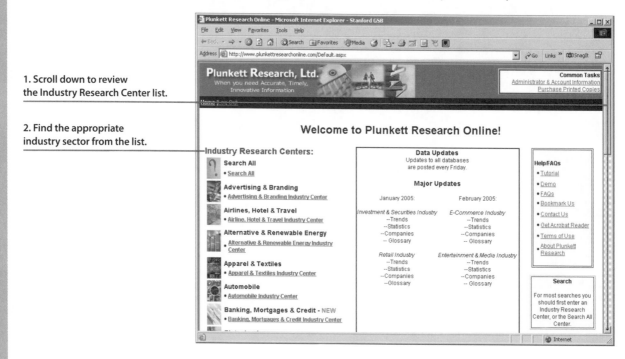

In this case, **Computers & Software** appears most relevant.

3. Under the **Computers & Software** heading, click **Infotech Industry Center**.

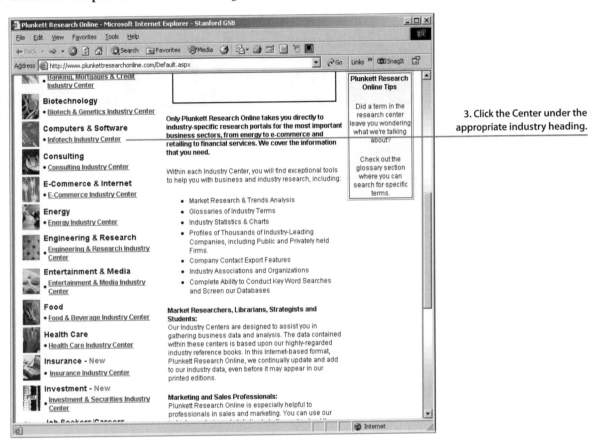

3. Click the Center under the appropriate industry heading.

This retrieves the Infotech Industry Center main page.

4. Select the button next to **Market Research and Trends**.

4. Select the button next to the type of data you need.

Result: A detailed report with recent history and major market trends in the Computers & Software sector.

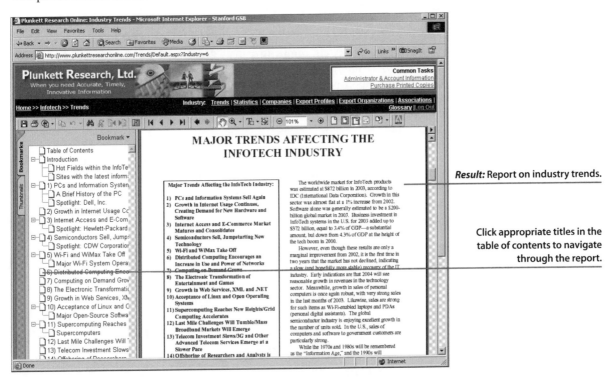

Result: Report on industry trends.

Click appropriate titles in the table of contents to navigate through the report.

■ Standard & Poor's NetAdvantage

Access at: College/university libraries.

Overview: NetAdvantage provides business and investment information for industry and company research, competitive intelligence, strategic planning, and many other purposes. Among its features, this resource allows for searching by NAICS codes and for exporting data into spreadsheet programs. (*Note:* The **NetAdvantage** definition of "industry" can be very broad, and may include some very different kinds of businesses, especially in newer or ill-defined industries.) For more on this resource and another sample search, see page 207.

Best for: Finding industry overview reports, particularly those focusing on publicly traded companies within that industry, locating key industry ratios and statistics, and finding trade publications.

SAMPLE SEARCHES

A. This first sample search uses **NetAdvantage** to find an overview of the publishing industry.

1. Under the **NetAdvantage** page header, click the **Industries** tab.

1. Click to access industry information.

On the **Industry Research** page, use the pull-down menu to find and select the most relevant industry topic.

2. Select **Publishing**.

3. Click the arrow to the right of the pull-down menu to go to the information.

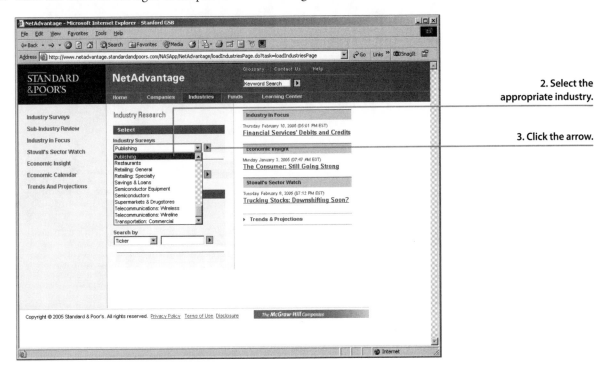

2. Select the appropriate industry.

3. Click the arrow.

Result: A general survey of the publishing industry. You can click report section links to access different topics, such as **Key Industry Ratios and Statistics**.

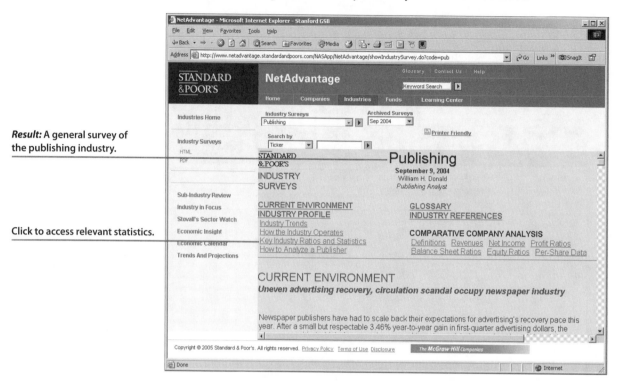

Result: A general survey of the publishing industry.

Click to access relevant statistics.

B. You can also use **NetAdvantage** to find information on subsectors of an industry. Here is a second sample search for subsectors of publishing.

On the home page, select the **Industries** tab under the **NetAdvantage** page header. (For more information, see the screen image on page 132.)

1. On the Industry Research page, select **Publishing** from the Industry Surveys pull-down menu.

2. Select **Publishing** again from the Sub-Industry Reviews pull-down menu directly below the first one.

3. Click the arrow next to the second pull-down menu to go to the review.

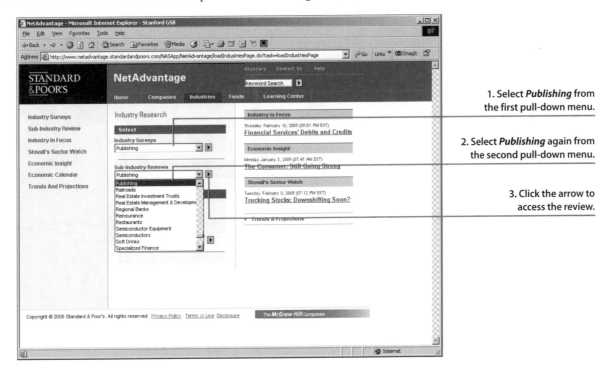

1. Select *Publishing* from the first pull-down menu.

2. Select *Publishing* again from the second pull-down menu.

3. Click the arrow to access the review.

Result: A publishing industry overview and forecast with a focus on subsectors within the industry. The review features separate predictions for newspaper publishing, book publishing, and other subsectors, and also covers subcategories within those subsectors (for example, academic and mass-market books).

Result: A publishing industry review and forecast.

Newspaper publishing subsector forecast.

Book publishing subsector predictions.

RESEARCHING AN INDUSTRY

ADDITIONAL FEE-BASED RESOURCES

◼ Factiva

Access at: *www.factiva.com* or college/university libraries.

Overview: Factiva, a joint venture between Dow Jones and Reuters, provides full-text access to a variety of newspaper, newswire, trade and business journal articles, in addition to public company financials and industry information. Find archived articles from major national and regional newspapers such as the *Wall Street Journal*, the *New York Times*, and the *Financial Times. (Note:* Full-text articles from the *LA Times, Chicago Tribune,* and *San Jose Mercury News* are no longer provided.) The site appears in the secondary resource section of this book because it can be difficult to access and certain areas are hard to use. (*Note:* If not accessed through a college or university library, the site usually charges a per article, monthly usage, or annual subscription fee and requires that you enter your user profile and your credit card information before beginning your search.)

Best for: Finding industry articles and financial information on companies.

◼ LexisNexis Statistical

Access at: College/university libraries.

Overview: LexisNexis Statistical is helpful for finding statistical information from the U.S. government, major international agencies, professional and trade organizations, commercial publishers, independent research organizations, universities, and other groups. You can search abstracts and more than 30,000 indexed tables provided by hundreds of government, international, and academic sources.

Best for: Locating industry numerical data (in table format).

◼ MultexNet

Access at: College/university libraries.

Overview: This resource, owned by Reuters, is designed primarily for investment professionals (such as stockbrokers and portfolio managers) and is particularly useful for determining how the financial community views specific industries. As a result, the information tends to lean toward industries dominated by publicly traded companies.

Best for: Finding financial, investment-related industry reports.

CHAPTER 16

Researching a Company

Conducting research about individual companies offers you many benefits, from identifying your biggest or toughest competitors to determining whether a potential customer is credit-worthy. If you're seeking funding for a business, prospective investors will certainly want to know about the health and performance of your major competitors.

Finding information about specific companies can often be difficult; after all, they don't necessarily want their competitors to know what they're up to. However, there is quite a bit of data available on publicly traded companies (that is, businesses that sell their stock on a public stock exchange). In the U.S., publicly traded companies are required by law to disclose financial information on a regular basis to the Securities and Exchange Commission.

As well, investment analysts track publicly traded companies for their investor clients, and you can access many of their reports on some of the databases listed in this book. These companies are usually of interest to the financial press, too, and you can also find articles about their performance in media archives (see pages 81-83).

While it is more difficult to find information about private and/or smaller companies, it's not impossible. Often you can collect information from industry publications and associations, local media in a company's home community, research companies such as Dun & Bradstreet, and even a company's own websites or customers.

Finding information about a company helps you:

- Learn which products and/or services a company offers and, often, how much they charge.
- Determine the revenues and profits of a company, sometimes including revenues for specific product lines.
- Gather background information about prospective customers and suppliers.
- Investigate potential strategic alliances by finding companies whose services and/or products complement yours.

Tips for Finding Company Information

1. Determine the correct name(s) of the company, including:

   ■ Its official corporate name. A company's corporate name may be different from the one you're familiar with. For instance, the corporate name for United Airlines is UAL Corporation.

   ■ The name of its parent or its subsidiary company or companies. Some corporations own many subsidiary companies. Macy's, Bloomingdale's, and Hecht's department stores are all subsidiaries of Federated Department Stores, Inc.

   ■ Its brand/product name(s). Often you will know a product's name but not the name of the company that makes it. For example, Crest toothpaste, Tide detergent, and Iams pet food are all made by Procter & Gamble.

2. Make sure you spell any names correctly when entering them into keyword searches.

3. Check the company's website(s). Look for an About Us section and/or a Press/Media section, which usually feature background information about the company and its officers, press releases, and recent news articles. Also look for product information and lists of clients/customers or testimonials.

4. Learn whether the company you're researching is public or private. If it is a publicly traded company, find the stock symbol used to identify that company. Try: *http://finance.yahoo.com/lookup*.

Other places to find information on publicly traded companies include:

   ■ EDGAR Database/U.S. Securities and Exchange Commission (see page 164)

   ■ Finance websites, such as Yahoo! Finance (see page 171)

   ■ Investment analysis sites including Standard and Poor's NetAdvantage (see pages 132 and 207) and Hoover's Online (see page 220)

Find information on private companies using resources such as:

   ■ A database listing businesses in a specific geographic area, such as ReferenceUSA (see page 156)

   ■ Dun & Bradstreet or other business credit reporting agencies (see page 220)

   ■ Articles about the company in local community newspapers, available through a variety of news databases and through the sites of individual newspapers

5. Identify the U.S. state in which the company is legally incorporated (if applicable). You can typically find the names of corporate officers and company contact information through the Secretary of State's office in the state where the company you're researching is incorporated.

■ Types of Company Information to Research

When searching for information on a company, focus on such issues as:

■ **Name(s) of the company:**
- Official corporate name
- Parent/subsidiary companies
- Product names
- Trademarks

■ **Company information:**
- Headquarters and location(s)
- Officers', executives', and staff names
- Press releases
- Product announcements

■ **Products/services of a company:**
- Leading product lines
- Pricing
- Features
- Distribution methods
- Patents/copyrights and other intellectual property

■ **Financial condition of the company, including:**
- Current revenues and profit figures
- Historical sales, financial performance, and growth rate
- Stock performance/market value
- Sales by product lines

■ **Other key issues:**
- Is the company publicly traded?
- Customers/client list/testimonials
- Legal/regulatory compliance issues

■ WORKSHEET: Company Research

Use this worksheet to record key information about the company you are researching.

■ Name(s) of the company

• Official corporate name

_____

_____

• Parent/subsidiary companies

_____

_____

• Product names

_____

_____

• Trademarks

_____

_____

■ Company information

• Headquarters and location(s)

_____

_____

• Officers', executives', and staff names

_____

_____

• Press releases

_____

_____

- Product announcements

_____

_____

■ **Products/services of a company**
- Leading product lines

_____

_____

- Pricing

_____

_____

- Features

_____

_____

- Distribution methods

_____

_____

- Patents/copyrights and other intellectual property

_____

_____

■ **Financial condition of the company, including:**
- Current revenues and profit figures

_____

_____

- Historical sales, financial performance, and growth rate

_____

_____

- Stock performance/market value

_____

_____

- Sales by product lines

_____

_____

■ **Other key issues:**
- Is the company publicly traded?

_____

_____

- Customers/client list/testimonials

_____

_____

_____

_____

- Legal/regulatory compliance issues

_____

_____

_____

_____

RESEARCHING A COMPANY

FREE RESOURCES

■ Business & Company Resource Center

Access at: Public and college/university libraries.

Overview: This resource is helpful for gathering general background information on companies, especially larger ones. In addition to company profiles, it also features links to articles focusing on areas such as management, financials, and operations, but depending on the company you are researching, you may not find many recent reports. **Business & Company Resource Center** is particularly helpful if you're looking for background on the origins and development of a company. For more on this resource and another sample search, see page 97.

Best For: Finding company information, especially on better-known businesses.

SAMPLE SEARCH

This search will locate a detailed profile of an existing computer training company.

Begin at the entry page.

1. Click the **Company** icon.

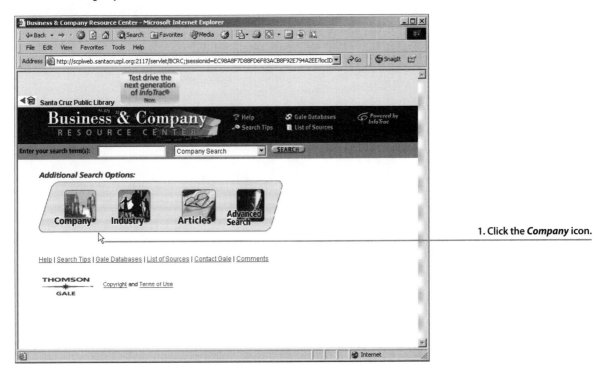

1. Click the *Company* icon.

The company search page appears.

2. Enter keywords for the name of the company (in this case, *New Horizons*).

3. Click **Search**.

2. Enter the company name keywords in the search field.

3. Click *Search*.

This retrieves a list of profiles on companies with the name *New Horizons*.

4. Click on the company name closest to that of the specific firm you're looking for.

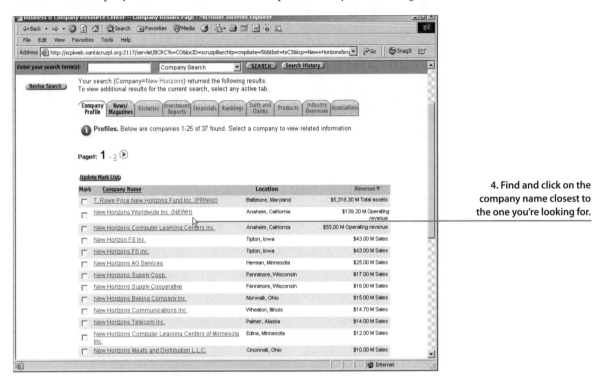

4. Find and click on the company name closest to the one you're looking for.

Result: A detailed company profile with links to articles on financial matters, management, product, operations, and other key company areas.

Result: Company profile with links to relevant articles

■ Company Websites

Access at: You can usually find a company's Web address through a major search engine such as Google or Yahoo!

Overview: Corporate websites offer a wealth of information on specific companies, from biographies of their executive teams to company news. If you're researching a competitor, that company's website is a great place to start.

Best for: Finding recent news on a company. Many company sites include a news or press section where they post press releases and articles about themselves.

SAMPLE SEARCH

Here's a sample search through the site of an existing computer training company for important news on the company.

1. Go to the company's website home page and look for a link to a **Press Room** or **Newsroom**. If there is no listing, look for a **Site Map**, usually near the bottom of the page, or try the **About Us** section. For this company, click **Site Map**.

1. Click *Site Map* to find the News section.

2. On the **Site Map**, under the **Company** heading, click **Newsroom**.

2. Click *Newsroom* for company information.

The **Newsroom** page that appears includes a general description of the company and both company-specific and industry news releases sorted by date.

3. Click the first (and most recent) press release.

Company description

Contact info

Corporate background info

3. Click the most recent press release.

Result: A press release announcing the company's partnership with a trade group to deliver new certified training courses. The release provides brief descriptions of the company and its partner and offers contact information for the company's spokesperson.

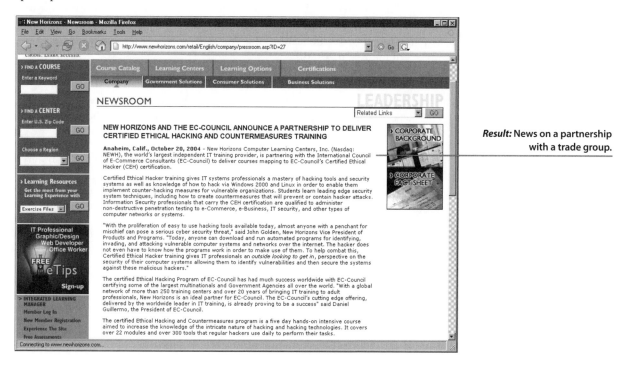

Result: News on a partnership with a trade group.

■ InfoTrac

Access at: Public and college/university libraries.

Overview: This popular database features millions of articles, mainly from magazines and reference books, from mainstream to more specialized sources. **InfoTrac** offers many journals and trade publications not available on other free sites, with some records reaching back to 1980.

Libraries have different ways of incorporating the **InfoTrac** database into their systems. Access to the database and search methods might vary from place to place. In general, look for a link to References and Databases on your library's home page. If you have difficulty finding it, ask your librarian for assistance.

The following sample search shows the **InfoTrac** interface used by the public library in Palo Alto, California. This first page appears when searching from the library or after entering your library card number when logging into the library site from a computer outside the library.

Best for: Locating hard-to-find articles on a company (that is, articles from trade publications).

SAMPLE SEARCH

The goal of the search is to find articles about a company, particularly those focusing on its executives.

1. On the **InfoTrac** search page, enter the company name in the **Keyword search** field. Put the phrase in quotation marks to eliminate irrelevant information on words used in the company name. (In this case, *"New Horizons Worldwide"* was used.)

2. From the options below the search field, select **in title, citation, abstract** to get articles that focus specifically on the company.

3. Click **Search**.

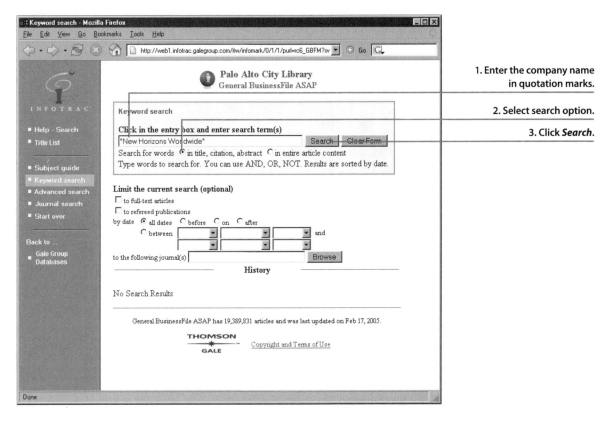

Your search results show a variety of articles along with their word counts. (This makes it easier to determine which are the longer, and possibly more comprehensive, articles.)

4. Since the goal of this sample search is to find information on who is running the company, click the first press release.

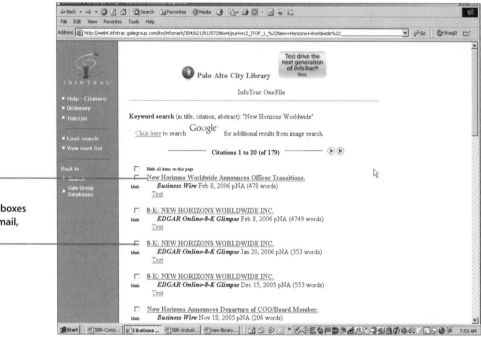

4. Click the title or text to read the article.

You can also use the checkboxes to mark articles to print, email, or retrieve later.

Result: The article retrieved reveals that the company is looking for a new chief executive officer (which could mean future changes in the company's operations and business direction).

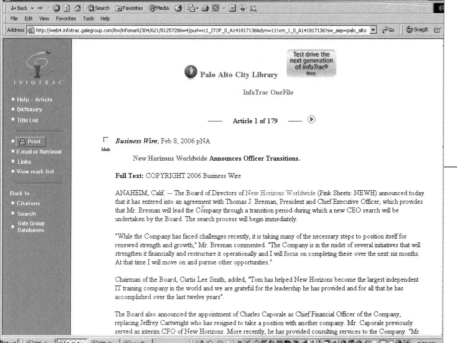

Result: A report that indicates the company is looking for a new CEO.

▪ ReferenceUSA

Access at: Public or college/university libraries.

Overview: ReferenceUSA makes a good starting point for identifying and finding information on companies, covering more than twelve million businesses in the U.S. and one million in Canada. You can use it to find the number of companies in a particular area, determine the strength of your competition, or learn about the background of a company. You may even find names, addresses, phone numbers, and other information about key company executives. **ReferenceUSA** also serves as a useful research tool for industry and target market data.

If your library carries **ReferenceUSA**, you can usually access it by following the links to references/databases and entering your library card number when prompted. If you are trying to enter from a computer outside the library and are presented with a window that asks for your name and password (instead of your library card number), this may have to do with the settings on your anti-virus software. Ask your reference librarian for assistance in adjusting the settings.

Best for: Finding information on companies in a particular U.S. region. Also good for building company and sales lists by industry or region.

SAMPLE SEARCH

Here's a sample search for a list of the computer training companies in Indianapolis, Indiana.

1. On the **ReferenceUSA** entry page, click **business data** (near the bottom).

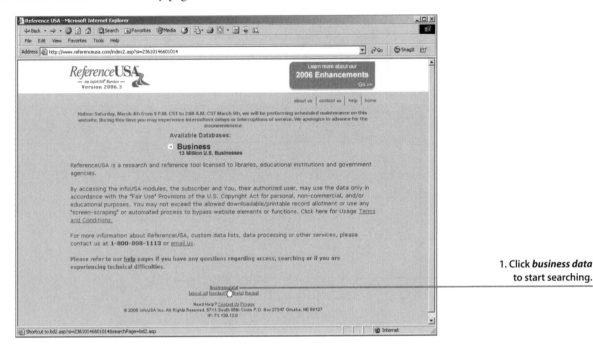

1. Click *business data* to start searching.

2. Click the **Custom Search** tab in the search window to access the appropriate search options.

2. Click the *Custom Search* tab to change search options.

Use the **Custom Search** page to select the characteristics you want to search by. This search will find companies in a particular metropolitan area, using the NAICS code for their industry. (For more information on NAICS codes and where to find them, see pages 25-27.)

3. Under **Yellow Pages (YP)**, check the box for **NAICS-2002**.

4. Under **Geography Selects**, check the box for **MSA (Metro Area)**.

5. Click **Create Search Form** to enter more specific search criteria and start searching.

3. Select the *NAICS* checkbox.

4. Select the *MSA (Metro Area)* checkbox.

5. Click *Create Search Form* to set more specific search criteria.

6. The **Search Criteria Fields** page that follows requests the NAICS code for the company's industry. In this case, the code for the computer training industry is 611420. If you don't know the code for the industry you're researching, click the NAICS codes links for a list. (*Note:* In this sample, the final digits of the code are omitted for a broader search. For more information on NAICS codes, see pages 25-27.)

6. Click to obtain an alphabetical list of NAICS codes (by industry name).

Click to obtain a numeric list of NAICS codes (by industry code number).

NAICS codes are listed in the pop-up window.

7. Enter the code in one of the boxes that asks for the NAICS code.

8. Use the scroll-down menu to select the state in which the MSA (metropolitan area) is located.

9. Click **Search Now!**

7. Enter the NAICS code here.

8. Select the state.

9. Click *Search Now!*

10. On the **Search Refinement** page that appears, use the scroll-down menu to select the metro area you want to include in your search (in this case, **Indianapolis, IN**).

11. Click **Search Now!**

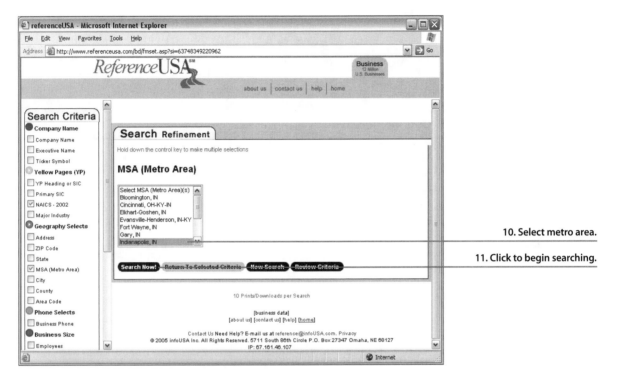

10. Select metro area.

11. Click to begin searching.

Result: A list of computer training companies in the greater Indianapolis metropolitan area.

12. You can also click on the name of a specific company to get more information about that company, as shown below.

Result: A list of computer training companies in the Indianapolis area.

12. Click a company name for more information.

Result: Detailed information on the company you selected, including number of employees, estimated sales, and credit rating.

Result: Listing provides detailed company information.

■ U.S. Securities and Exchange Commission: EDGAR Database

Access at: *http://www.sec.gov/edgar.shtml*

Overview: As all public companies, national and global, active in U.S. markets must file their financial information with the SEC, its EDGAR (Electronic Data Gathering, Analysis, and Retrieval system) database serves as a primary source of investment information. The database works best when you are looking for information on a specific company. *Note:* Much of this information can also be found on other free investment sites, such as Yahoo! Finance (see page 171).

Best for: Gathering investment and other financial information on specific public companies.

SAMPLE SEARCH

This search will investigate the latest investment information filings from a leading computer training company.

1. Start at the SEC EDGAR home page, and click **Search for Company Filings**.

1. Click to find recent company filings.

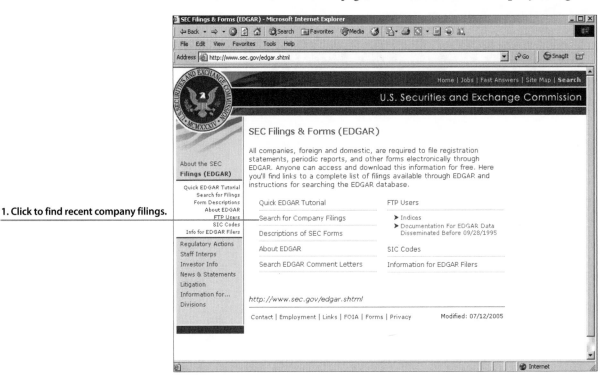

2. On the next window, click **Companies & Other Filers**.

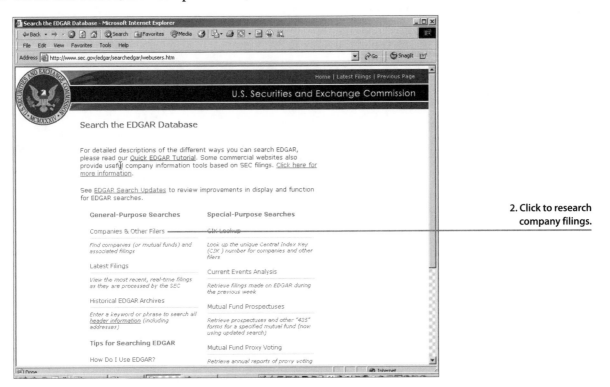

2. Click to research company filings.

3. In the search field on the next page, enter keywords for the company name (in this case, *learning tree*).

4. Select the **Include** ownership forms option for the broadest search.

5. Click the **Find Companies** button to start your search.

3. Enter company name keywords.

4. Select *Include*.

5. Click *Find Companies*.

The window that appears shows all filings for Learning Tree International Inc.

6. Click **html** (or **text**) to display specifics on the item filed.

6. Click for details on a filing.

List shows all company filings.

The next window shows a description of the filing, as well as the identity of the person and organization responsible for the filing.

7. Click one of the links under "Document" to read the actual document filed. (*Note:* Both links shown here lead to the same document.)

7. Click to read the filed document.

The information window shows the nature of the filing and by whom it was filed.

The eight-page legal document that appears shows changes in the ownership of company stock.

8. Scroll down to find details on the reason for the filing.

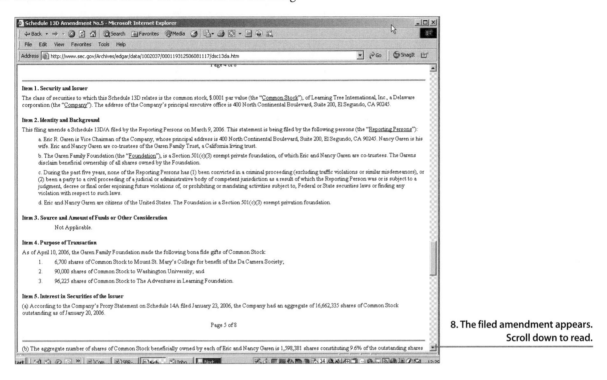

8. The filed amendment appears.
Scroll down to read.

Result: The document reveals that the amendment was filed because the owners of Learning Tree donated shares to various organizations.

Result: Document reveals that an amendment was filed to reflect recently donated shares.

■ Yahoo! Finance

Access at: *http://finance.yahoo.com*

Overview: Yahoo! Finance offers several varieties of stock-market-related information on companies, from ticker symbols to growth charts. It also compiles company news from various sources (Reuters, Business Wire, Associated Press, Motley Fool) under its Headlines section for each company.

Best for: Finding stock-market-related company information.

SAMPLE SEARCH

This sample search will locate financial information on an existing computer training company. While there are other ways to search, the method shown here takes you directly to the company's financial information page.

1. Go to the **Yahoo! Finance** home page, and click **Symbol Lookup** next to the **Get Quotes** search field. (*Note:* If you already know a company's stock exchange ticker symbols, you can skip this step.)

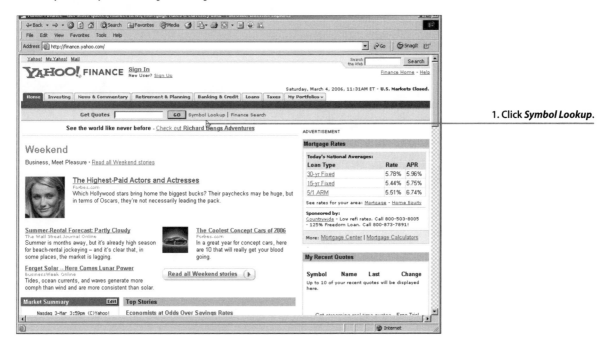

1. Click *Symbol Lookup*.

2. On the **Symbol Lookup** page, enter the company name in the search field (in this case, *Learning Tree*).

3. Click the **Look Up** button.

2. Enter the company name in the search field.

3. Click the *Look Up* button.

The results show the company's symbol, the stock exchange it is listed on, and its industry classification.

4. Click the company's stock symbol.

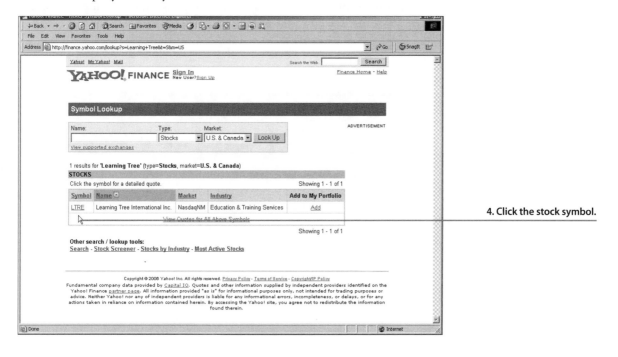

4. Click the stock symbol.

Clicking the company's stock symbol retrieves a company's stock listing page that includes a financial summary, news releases, a growth chart, and plenty of other financial information.

The **Headlines** section, which features news and press releases on the company, appears about midway down the page.

5. Scroll down to view the titles and click the press release on the company's financials.

5. Click the press release on company financials.

Result: A quarterly income statement for the company. This could be quite useful if you're trying to assess company stability, growth, and potential.

Result: A detailed quarterly income statement.

RESEARCHING A COMPANY

ADDITIONAL FREE RESOURCES

■ Business media websites

Access at: Some of the major sites include **BusinessWeek Online** (*www.businessweek.com*), **MarketWatch.com** (*www.marketwatch.com*), the **New York Times Online** (*www.nytimes. com*), and the **Wall Street Journal Online** (*www.wsj.com*). You can find other business media websites through major search engines such as Google and Yahoo!

Overview: Business media websites provide an excellent resource for up-to-date and comprehensible company information (articles are written for the mainstream, not necessarily for analysts). You can usually find daily and archived articles written about a company through each site's search function. (*Note:* Many of these sites will charge for accessing articles published more than one week earlier.)

Best for: Finding up-to-date, easy-to-access company news and financial developments.

■ Business Wire

Access at: *www.businesswire.com*

Overview: Business Wire disseminates news announcements from thousands of companies worldwide. It is a good source for business news generated by the companies themselves. Public relations and investor relations departments use **Business Wire** to release their companies' breaking news, earnings results, product announcements, mergers and acquisitions, legal issues, press conference announcements, and more. (*Note:* **Business Wire** only lists press releases from the past thirty days.)

Best for: Gathering up-to-date, company-sanctioned business news.

■ PR Newswire

Access at: *www.prnewswire.com*

Overview: PR Newswire is an up-to-the-minute database of all news releases provided by company and PR agencies and sent over the wire during the past thirty days. More than 40,000 companies are listed. **PR Newswire** allows you to search by industry, company, and topic. As with Business Wire, releases are listed for only thirty days.

Best for: Locating current company-sanctioned news and press releases.

■ U.S. Patent and Trademark Office

Access at: *www.uspto.gov*

Overview: The **U.S. Patent and Trademark Office** provides public access to its database of registered patents and trademarks over the Web. This information is especially helpful when developing a potentially competitive product or trying to find a name or slogan for your own company. Doing your homework here may help you avoid a legal patent- or trademark-infringement quagmire later.

Best for: Researching patents and trademarks held by potential competitors or other companies; avoiding potential patent and trademark disputes.

Part IV: STRAIGHT TO THE NUMBERS YOU NEED

NOTES:

RESEARCHING A COMPANY

FEE-BASED RESOURCES

▮ EBSCO's Business Source Complete

Access at: College/university libraries.

Overview: With a little searching on **Business Source Complete**, you can tap into detailed reports on a particular company (especially larger, better known businesses) or industry. The resource features the full text of more than 2,400 scholarly business publications, including the *Harvard Business Review* and *MIT Sloan Management Review.*

Best for: Finding comprehensive business reports on a particular company.

SAMPLE SEARCH

This search uncovers an in-depth report on an existing national computer training company.

1. On the home page, under **Browse**, click **Company Profiles**.

1. Click *Company Profiles.*

2. In the search field, enter keywords for the name of the company that interests you (in this case, *Learning Tree*).

3. Click **Browse**.

2. Enter the company name.

3. Click *Browse*.

A profile and report on the company Learning Tree International appears in
the results.

4. Click the company name link.

4. Click the company name.

This retrieves an overview of the company, including location/contact information, a NAICS code, an abstract (description), and a list of products and services.

5. Click the **Datamonitor Report** link at the top of the overview.

5. Click *Datamonitor Report*.

Company overview

Result: A comprehensive fourteen-page report in PDF form. The report includes detailed information on the business, including company history, competitors, and key employee biographies.

You can easily navigate this report using the **Table of Contents** links in the left-hand column. You can also download the report to your computer.

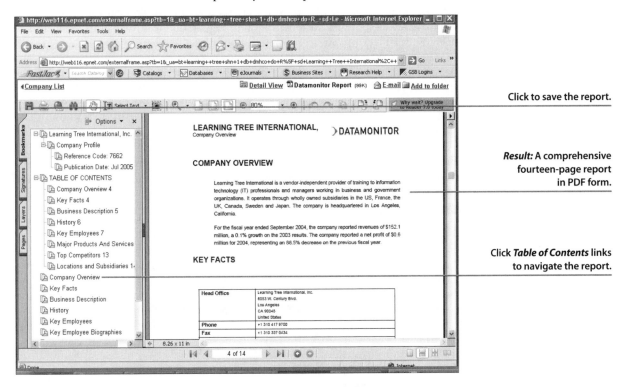

Click to save the report.

Result: A comprehensive fourteen-page report in PDF form.

Click *Table of Contents* links to navigate the report.

■ LexisNexis AlaCarte!

Access at: *http://alacarte.lexisnexis.com*

Overview: **LexisNexis** offers Internet searches on more than 20,000 sources containing over 3.8 billion documents, some dating as far back as 1968. A big plus is its pay-as-you-go format, which lets you search for documents and pay for the ones you want by credit card, with no subscription or registration fees. One of its drawbacks, however, is its lack of abstracts or descriptions of the articles you can retrieve through your searches. You may have to buy an article to see what's in it.

Before you search, you need to register on the site by clicking the registration link on the home page. You are given the option of putting in your credit card information during registration or entering it later, after you have selected a document to purchase. Once you register, the system will return you to the home page.

Best for: **LexisNexis** is especially good for finding updated company market share information and hard-to-find transcripts from major television and radio broadcasts.

SAMPLE SEARCH

The search will locate market-share information on a computer industry leader.

1. Click the **Business Intelligence** tab on the menu at the top of the home page to retrieve the **Business Intelligence** search page.

1. Click the *Business Intelligence* tab.

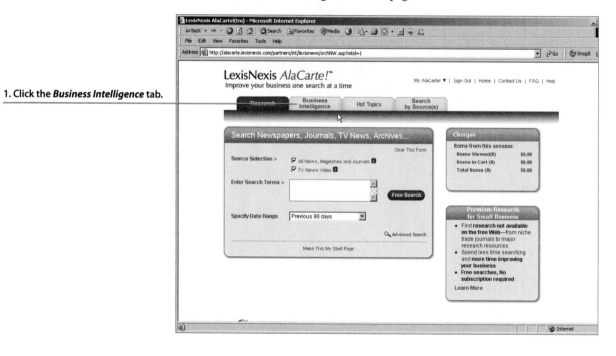

2. On the **Business Intelligence** search page, enter your search keywords (in this case, *New Horizons Worldwide market share*).

3. You can narrow or expand your source selection using the checkboxes above the search field.

4. Use the pull-down menu below the search field to specify your time frame.

5. Click **Free Search**.

6. When the **Online Search Results** appear, use the checkboxes to select the article(s) most likely to give you the information you need.

7. Click **Add to Cart** at the top of the page to put any articles in your shopping cart for purchase when your search is complete.

Result: A market guide profile of the computer training company (not shown).

6. Select a relevant article.

7. Click *Add to Cart* to buy.

■ MultexNet

Access at: College/university libraries.

Overview: This resource, owned by Reuters, is designed primarily for investment professionals (that is, stockbrokers, portfolio managers, and the like) and is particularly useful in determining how the financial community views specific companies or industries. As a result, the information tends to lean towards publicly traded companies and industries dominated by public companies. (*Note:* Goldman Sachs and Merrill Lynch are two investment banks not included on this site.)

Best for: Analyst reports on publicly traded companies.

SAMPLE SEARCH

This sample search will seek financial analysis of reports on computer training companies.

1. On the home page, enter the search term *computer training* in the **Keywords** field.

2. Select your keyword search parameters from the options below the search field.

3. Click the **Research Categories** pull-down menu and select **Industry Reports** to narrow your search.

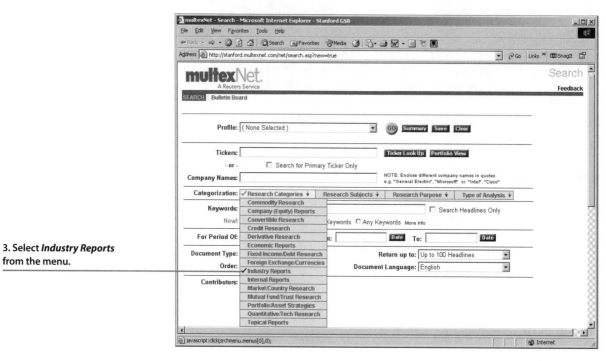

3. Select *Industry Reports* from the menu.

4. Use the various scroll menus on the resulting page to narrow the search further. (You may be able to find your specific industry and company using these menus.) In this case, select **North America** from the **Regions** menu and **United States** from the **Countries** menu (both near the bottom of the page).

5. Click **Go** to search.

4. Use scrolling menus to narrow search by location.

5. Click *Go* to search.

The search results offer reports on a number of leading computer training companies and on the computer training industry as a whole.

6. Scroll down the page to find and select an analysts' report on a specific company (in this case, **New Horizons Worldwide**).

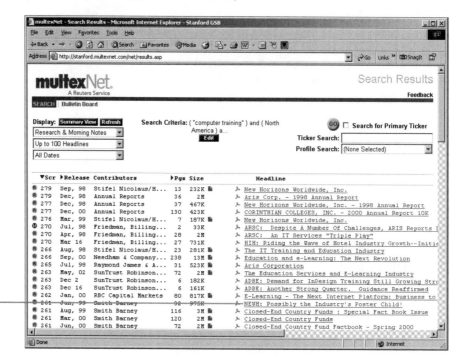

6. Select report on computer training industry leader.

Result: An analysts' report on a computer training industry leader. Navigate through the report using the section headers feature.

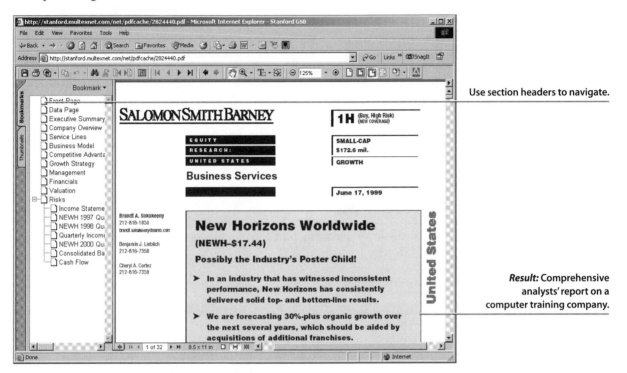

Use section headers to navigate.

Result: Comprehensive analysts' report on a computer training company.

▓ OneSource U.S. Business Browser

Access at: College/university libraries.

Summary: This resource is particularly useful when you're looking for data on a particular company, especially a larger one. Information includes location and contact details, number of employees, financials (which can be downloaded into an Excel spreadsheet), executive biographies, analyst reports, and much more. You can also find a sampling of the companies in a certain industry in a particular geographic area. For this second purpose, this resource is slightly more awkward to use. However, it does provide a comprehensive body of information on the companies it profiles.

Best for: Finding detailed company information, especially on larger public and private corporations.

SAMPLE SEARCHES

A. The first sample search will find computer training companies in the Indianapolis, Indiana, area.

1. Start at the home page, and click **Companies** about midway down the page.

1. Click *Companies.*

The **Find Companies** window appears.

2. In the **Search Variables** area, under **Location**, click **Metro Area.**

2. Click *Metro Area*.

3. Under **Metro Area Search Criteria**, use the **States** scroll-down menu to find and select **IN** for Indiana. This displays cities in Indiana in the scroll-down menu to the right.

4. Select **Indianapolis, Indiana**.

5. Choose the **Search on the selected Metro Area** option.

6. Click the **Search** button at the top or bottom of the window.

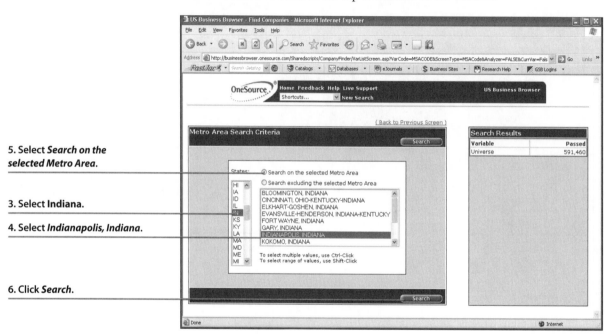

5. Select *Search on the selected Metro Area*.

3. Select *Indiana*.

4. Select *Indianapolis, Indiana*.

6. Click *Search*.

On the next window, note that the **Search Results** column on the right-hand side shows 2,770 companies listed in Indianapolis.

7. Back in the **Search Variables** box, click **Primary Industry**.

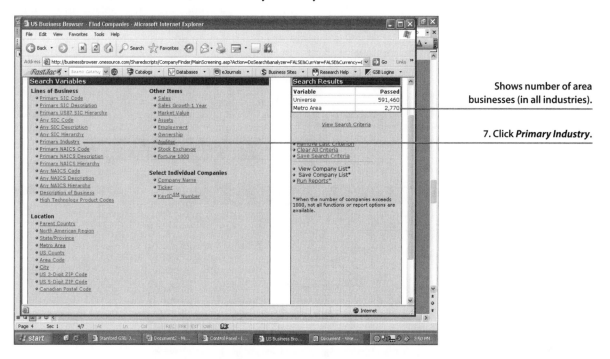

Shows number of area businesses (in all industries).

7. Click *Primary Industry*.

A selection menu appears.

8. Make sure the **Search on the selected Primary Industry** option is selected.

9. Click the industry closest to that of the companies you're looking for (in this case, **Computer Services**).

10. Click **Search**.

8. Make sure first option is selected.

9. Choose *Computer Services*.

10. Click *Search*.

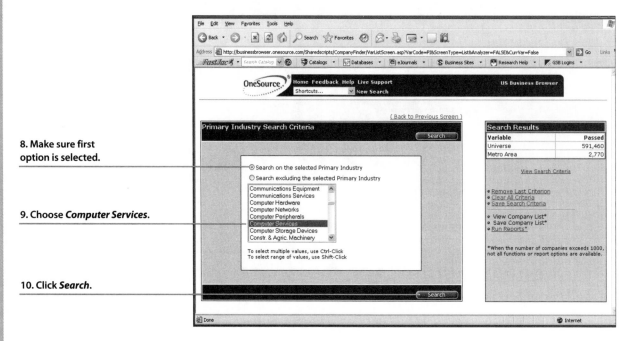

Note in the **Search Results** field that this retrieves nine companies in the Indianapolis area.

11. Click **View Company List** under the **Search Results** field.

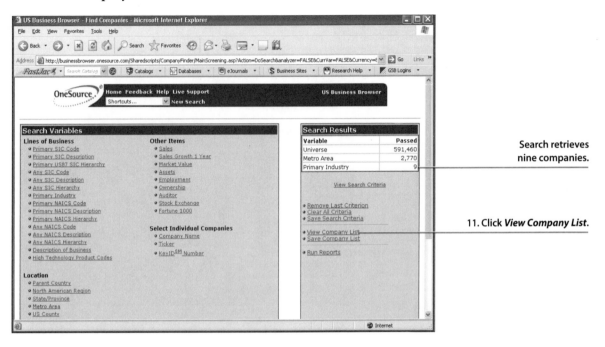

Search retrieves
nine companies.

11. Click *View Company List*.

This next window gives the names of nine computer services businesses.

12. Click a company name (or select the checkbox and click on **Get Info**) for a detailed profile.

12. Click a company name for additional information.

Result: None of the companies on the list, including the one displayed below, is in the computer training field. The range of industries under the Computer Services category here spans the field from maintenance and repair to data processing and preparation. This may indicate that there is room for a computer services company in the area, but it could also mean there isn't a market for it. Be sure to check other resources before drawing your conclusions.

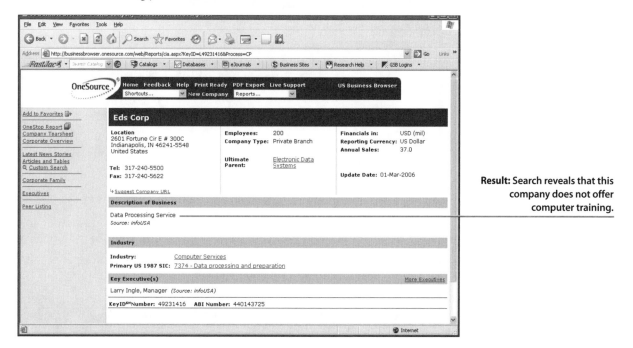

Result: Search reveals that this company does not offer computer training.

B. This search will locate detailed information on national computer training companies. (*Note:* In addition to that goal, this search is also designed to demonstrate some of **OneSource**'s NAICS-related features.)

1. On the home page, click **Companies**.

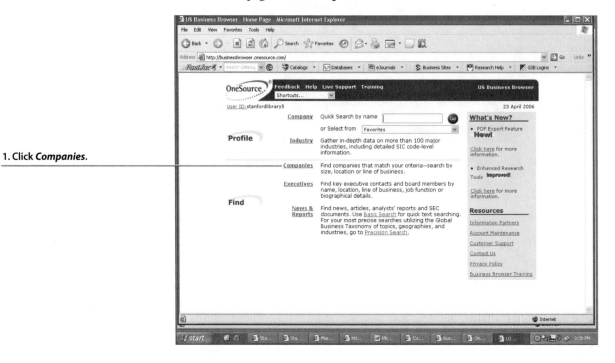

1. Click *Companies*.

The **Find Companies** window appears.

2. Under **Search Variables**, click **Primary NAICS Description**.

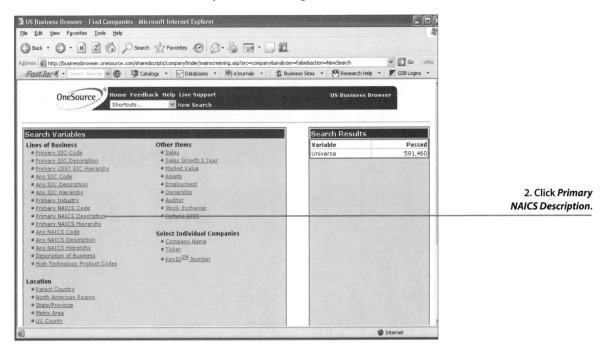

2. Click *Primary NAICS Description*.

In the **Primary NAICS Description Search Criteria** window that appears:

3. Enter relevant keywords (*computer training*) into the search field.

4. Select the **NAICS Brief Description** option.

5. Click **Search**.

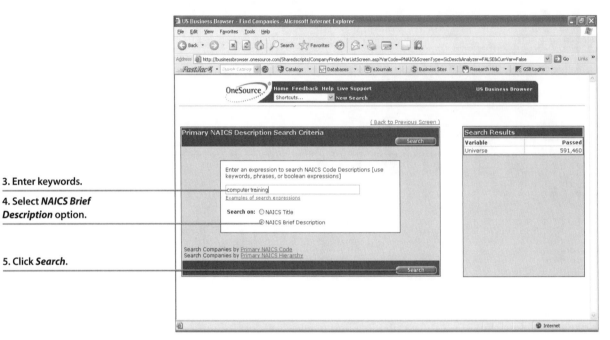

3. Enter keywords.

4. Select *NAICS Brief Description* option.

5. Click *Search*.

In the next window, under **Primary NAICS Description Search Criteria**:

6. Select the check box next to **Computer Training**.

7. Click **Search**.

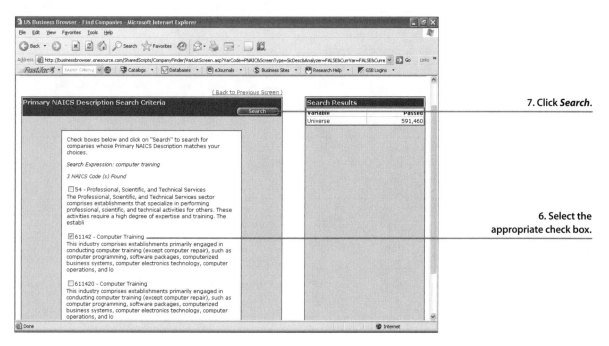

The **Search Results** field in the window to the right shows nine companies at the national level that fit the NAICS description.

8. Click **View Company List**.

Search highlights nine computer training companies.

8. Click *View Company List*.

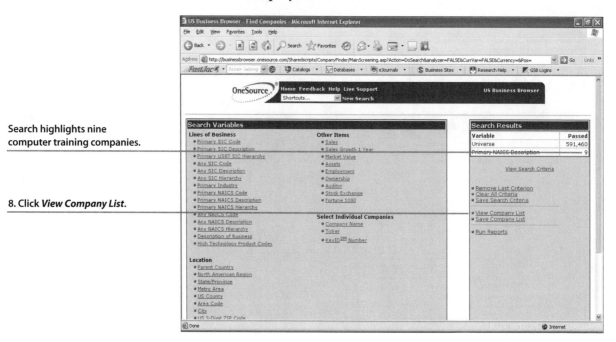

The next window gives the names of nine computer training companies in the U.S.

9. Click a company name (or select the checkbox and click on **Get Info**) for a detailed profile.

9. Click a company name for more information.

Result: A detailed company profile appears.

The NAICS code search at the national level led to a comprehensive body of information on a computer training industry leader, including location and contact information, exportable financials, executive biographies, news stories, and analyst reports.

Contact Information

Executive biographies

Company financials

Result: A detailed company profile.

■ Standard & Poor's NetAdvantage

Access at: College/university libraries.

Overview: In addition to providing solid business and investment information for industry analysis, S&P's **NetAdvantage** also serves as a good resource for company research and competitive intelligence. As it is stock market oriented, its focus is on public companies. For more on this resource and another sample search, see page 132.

Best for: Locating reports and financial information on publicly traded companies.

SAMPLE SEARCH

The goal of this sample search is to find detailed financial information (that is, numbers) on a public company (and computer industry leader). Start at the home page.

1. Under **Publication Search**, use the **Select publication** pull-down menu to choose **Company Profile**.

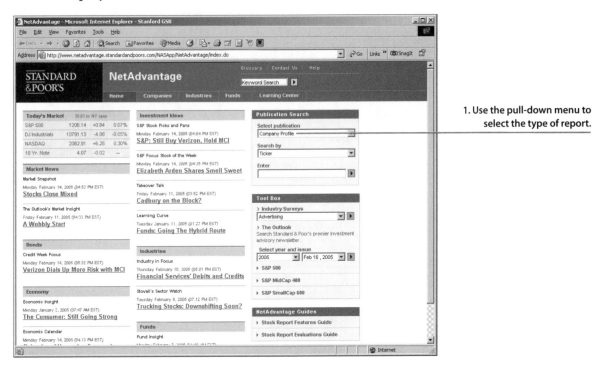

1. Use the pull-down menu to select the type of report.

2. From the **Search by** pull-down menu, select **Company Name**.

3. Enter the name of the company in the **Enter** search field (in this case, *New Horizons Worldwide*).

4. Click the **Go** button to retrieve results.

2. From the *Search by* pull-down menu, select *Company Name*.

3. Enter the name of the company.

4. Click *Go* to get reports.

NetAdvantage returns a business summary on the company.

5. To find numerical data, click **Financials** from the list of reports on the left side of the page.

5. Click *Financials*.

Company profile.

Result: Detailed revenue and earnings information in a table format.

(*Note:* You can click on **Register** in the left-hand column for a list of company executives.)

Result: Report shows annual revenue, earnings, and income data.

◼ Thomson One Banker Analytics

Access at: College/university libraries.

Overview: Thomson provides a good source for finding detailed investment data on specific businesses, with information on more than 65,000 companies internationally. The information it offers includes key financials and growth rates, analyst forecasts, merger and acquisition information, SEC filings, and comparisons with comparable companies (or "peers"). Data can be downloaded to an Excel spreadsheet for further analysis.

Best for: Finding sophisticated investment-related information on a particular company. It's most useful for those well versed in stock terminology and measures.

SAMPLE SEARCH

This search will locate detailed financial information on a large computer training company and will download it to an Excel spreadsheet.

1. When accessing the database from a university library, you will first see the **Company Overview** window with various search and navigation options.

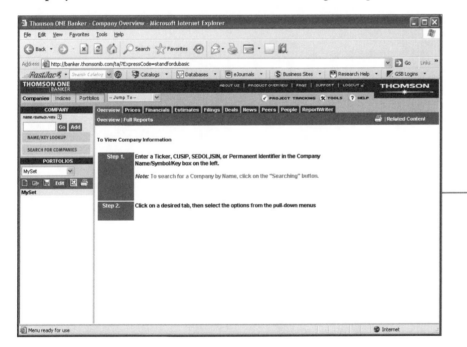

1. Search begins at *Company Overview* window.

2. Enter a company name in the search field in the left-hand column (in this case, *new horizons*).

3. Click **Go**.

2. Enter a company name in the field.

3. Click *Go*.

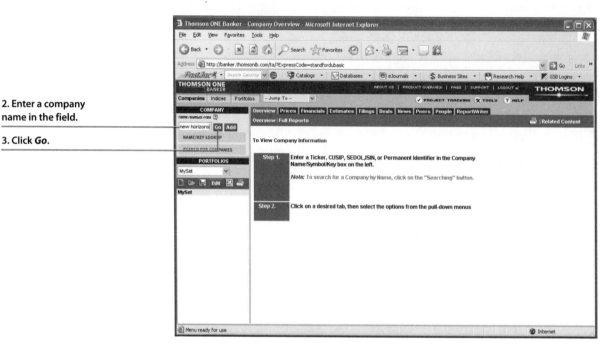

The next window presents a detailed overview of the company.

4. Click the **Peers** tab just above the overview information.

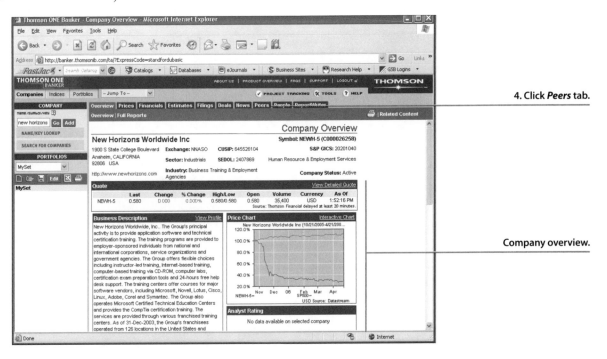

4. Click *Peers* tab.

Company overview.

A list of company competitors appears in the left-hand column. The report section to the right shows detailed financial comparison with peers.

5. Click a company name in the left-hand column.

5. Click a competitor's name from the list.

Report compares company financials with competitors.

In the next window, the competitor's (or peer's) financial information is highlighted at the top of the page.

Financial information for selected peer now appears at the top.

New Horizons information now displays with that of other peers.

6. Click the **People** tab at the top of the page.

6. Click *People*.

This retrieves a list of company officers and directors.

7. Click the **Financials** tab.

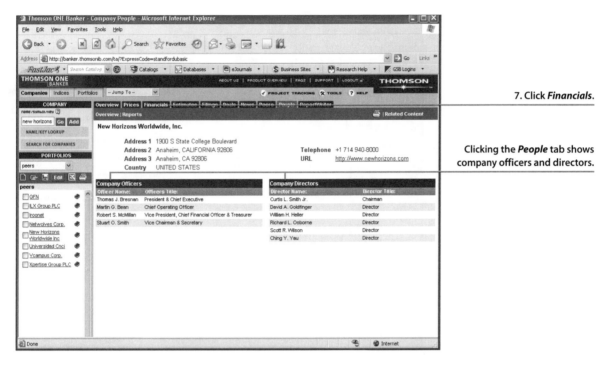

7. Click *Financials*.

Clicking the *People* tab shows
company officers and directors.

The next window provides a detailed annual financial report on New Horizons.

8. Click the **Excel** icon to export the data.

8. Click *Excel* icon to export data.

Detailed financial
data on New Horizons.

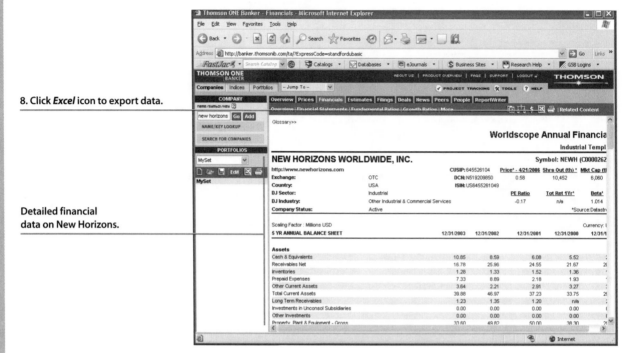

A window will appear asking if you want to open or save the file. It's usually safer to save the file.

9. In the File Download box, click **Save**.

9. Click *Save* to download
the file to your computer.

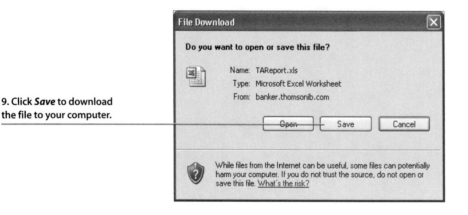

10. Open your **Excel** program and use the **Excel** file menu to find the New Horizons data file and open it from within the program, as shown below. Save the file.

Result: You have retrieved and saved a large and useful body of information, including peer comparisons, names of company officers and directors, and detailed financials.

10. Use the Excel file menu to find the New Horizons data on your computer and save the final file.

Result: Data has been exported to and saved on your Excel spreadsheet.

	A	B	C	D	E	F	G	H

Worldscope Annual Financials

Industrial Template

NEW HORIZONS WORLDWIDE, INC. Symbol: NEWH (C000026258)

http://www.newhorizons.com			CUSIP: 645526104	Price³ - 4/21/2006	Shrs Out (th) ³	Mkt Cap (th) ³
Exchange:	OTC		DCN: N519209850	0.58	10,452	6,060
Country:	USA		ISIN: US6455261049			
DJ Sector:	Industrial			PE Ratio	Tot Ret 1Yr³	Beta³
DJ Industry:	Other Industrial & Commercial Services			-0.17	#N/A	1.01
Company Status:	Active					*Source:Datastream

Scaling Factor : Millions USD Currency: USD

5 YR ANNUAL BALANCE SHEET			12/31/2003	12/31/2002	12/31/2001	12/31/2000	12/31/1999
Assets							
Cash & Equivalents			10.85	8.59	6.08	5.52	2.87
Receivables Net			16.78	25.96	24.55	21.67	20.99
Inventories			1.28	1.33	1.52	1.36	1.23
Prepaid Expenses			7.33	8.89	2.18	1.93	1.44
Other Current Assets			3.64	2.21	2.91	3.27	3.32
Total Current Assets			39.88	46.97	37.23	33.75	29.84
Long Term Receivables			1.23	1.35	1.20	#N/A	2.11
Investments in Unconsol Subsidiaries			0.00	0.00	0.00	0.00	0.00

Sheet1

Ready NUM

RESEARCHING A COMPANY

ADDITIONAL FEE-BASED RESOURCES

◼ ABI/INFORM Global (from ProQuest)

Access at: College/university libraries.

Overview: This resource indexes and abstracts journal articles in the areas of business conditions, trends, management techniques, corporate strategies, and industry-specific topics worldwide. The database features information on 60,000 companies and covers nearly 1,800 leading business and management periodicals, including respected journals such as *Journal of Business Ethics* and *Journal of the Academy of Marketing*. You can also retrieve full articles from the *Wall Street Journal*, the only newspaper on the database.

Best for: Finding articles about companies and competition from hard-to-find trade publications, business journals, and the *Wall Street Journal*.

◼ Dun & Bradstreet

Access at: *www.dnb.com*

Overview: This site offers a vast amount of financial and market information on virtually any businesses you could research. There are thousands of financial reports on potential partners, suppliers, and competitors. The reports vary in price and cover everything from credit history reports to investigations of a company's background to check for the presence and value of any suits, liens, or judgments.

Best for: Locating comprehensive financial data on companies.

◼ Hoover's Online

Access at: *www.hoovers.com* or college/university libraries.

Overview: You can access some useful company information, from company overviews to biographies of key executives, for free by going directly to **Hoover's** website. Much of the detailed financial data, however, is only available to subscribers or academic library users. **Hoover's** is best known as a resource for financial information, including SEC filings. You can also use it to compare companies within an industry. In general, although much of the information it offers can be found elsewhere, **Hoover's** compiles and presents data to users in an easily accessible format.

Best for: Finding financial information on publicly traded companies.

■ Mergent

Access at: *www.mergentonline.com*

Overview: Mergent provides access to detailed corporate financial histories and real-time SEC filings for more than 11,000 U.S. public companies and real-time SEC filings for more than 17,000 non-U.S. companies. Filings date back to 1993 and are searchable by company name, ticker symbol, filing date, and filing type. Other reports include company synopses, highlights, history, joint ventures, business, subsidiaries, long-term debt, and management executives. Conduct a search by NAICS code, geographic region, number of employees, and other factors.

Best for: Comparing the financial criteria of one company to financials for others in the same industry.

CHAPTER 17

Researching a Target Market

Understanding your customers is essential to business success. You need to know who they are, where they are, what they want, how they behave, and what they can afford. Most importantly, you have to know that they exist—and in numbers big enough to support your business.

If you are seeking financing for your company, anticipate that your investors are going to grill you about the size of your potential target market. They will want to know that this market is large enough to sustain your business, even in the face of existing competition.

Your target market may be either consumers (in which case yours is a B-to-C, or business-to-consumer, business) or other businesses (a B-to-B, or business-to-business, business). In either case, before you begin to research your target market, you must narrow the market definition even more by identifying the particular market segment you want to reach.

You can segment your target market by factors including:

■ **Consumer Customers**

- Age range
- Income level
- Educational level
- Home ownership
- Occupation
- Marital status/household size
- Ethnic/religious group
- Location
- Psychographic (personality traits, purchasing preferences, and so on)
- Other common traits

■ **Business Customers**

- Industry

- Location

- Number of employees

- Revenue level

- Business stage and age

- Other common traits

Finding target market information helps you:

■ Determine the size of a market and whether it is large enough to sustain your business successfully

■ Understand the characteristics of your potential customers, what motivates them, what they buy, and where and how they buy

■ Gain insight into the trends affecting your target market so you are better prepared to respond to future changes in the market

Tips for Finding Target Market Information

1. One of the best places to start looking for target market data is at one of the U.S. Census Bureau's websites. Census Bureau data is free and detailed. It's also easy to access through sites like American FactFinder: *http://factfinder.census.gov/ home/saff/main.html*. Here you can quickly find a wide range of population data at the national, state, metropolitan region, and zip code levels. See pages 231 and 232 for more information on American FactFinder, and other sites that offer U.S. Census Bureau data.

2. Another easy-to-use free site that delivers statistical data on target markets is Sperling's BestPlaces (see page 254).

3. The most detailed insights about target markets are often compiled by private research firms. Their data can be expensive to acquire. However, a few resources, such as Mintel (see page 263) and Marketresearch.com (see page 272), are both available for free through many college or university libraries.

4. If your target market consists of businesses in a specific industry, you can typically gather a great deal of information from the trade association serving that industry. For instance, if you sell commercial kitchen equipment, your target market may be restaurants, and you can find information about the number and growth rate of restaurants at the National Restaurant Association's website. For a list of industry associations see: *www.PlanningShop.com/ associations*.

5. If your target market consists of individuals with specific demographic characteristics, such as members of a specific ethnic group or religion, you can often find associations serving that group. If your market consists of consumers with specific interests or hobbies, such as gardening or travel, you can typically find associations serving those consumers, as well. These social organizations often have access to statistics about the size and growth rate of their constituents.

6. Many media outlets (including magazines, newspapers, radio and television stations) that serve a specific market offer details about their target markets in their information for advertisers. Check their websites.

7. If you're seeking demographic data on a geographic target market, you've got access to a large amount of free data from the U.S. Government, particularly the U.S. Census Bureau: *www.census.gov*.

Types of Target Market Information to Research

When searching for information on a target market, focus on such issues as:

GENERAL SIZE OF MARKET

- What is the approximate size of the target market?
- What is the historic rate of growth of the target market?
- What changes are occurring that could affect the size of the market (including income levels, need for product/service, social values)?
- What are forecasts for growth of the market?

DEMOGRAPHICS

Define objective characteristics of likely customers:

- **Consumer Customers**
  - Age range
  - Income level
  - Educational level
  - Home ownership
  - Marital status/household size
  - Ethnic/religious group
  - Occupation

- **Business Customers**
  - Industries
  - Revenue level
  - Number of employees
  - Business stage/age

GEOGRAPHIC FACTORS

Define the geographic area you intend to serve:

- What is the overall population of the target geographic area?
- What is the overall economic health of that geographic area?
- How many people or businesses in that geographic area fit the characteristics of likely customers?
- How many companies in the same line of business already exist in that geographic area?
- What are the size and profile of the workforce in that geographic area?

PSYCHOGRAPHIC FACTORS

Describe the psychographic characteristics of likely customers—and the size of the market with those characteristics—including:

- Purchasing patterns (where and how they shop)
- Hobbies
- Recreational activities
- Publications/media read/watched
- Social/political philosophy (that is, conservative/liberal)
- Orientation to technology (that is, technophobe, early adopter)
- Other

■ WORKSHEET: Target Market Research

When searching for information on a target market, focus on such issues as:

GENERAL SIZE OF MARKET

■ What is the approximate size of the target market?

_____

■ What is the historic rate of growth of the target market?

_____

■ What changes are occurring that could affect the size of the market (including income levels, need for product/service, social values)?

_____

_____

_____

_____

_____

_____

■ What are forecasts for growth of the market?

_____

_____

_____

_____

_____

_____

_____

DEMOGRAPHICS

Define objective characteristics of likely customers:

■ **Consumer Customers**

• Age range

_____

• Income level

_____

• Educational level

_____

• Home ownership

_____

• Marital status/household size

_____

• Ethnic/religious group

_____

• Occupation

_____

■ **Business Customers**

• Industries

_____

• Revenue level

_____

• Number of employees

_____

• Business stage/age

_____

GEOGRAPHIC FACTORS

Define the geographic area you intend to serve:

■ What is the overall population of the target geographic area?

_____

■ What is the overall economic health of that geographic area?

_____

■ How many people or businesses in that geographic area fit the characteristics of likely customers?

_____

■ How many companies in the same line of business already exist in that geographic area?

_____

■ What are the size and profile of the workforce in that geographic area?

_____

PSYCHOGRAPHIC FACTORS

Describe the psychographic characteristics of likely customers—and the size of the market with those characteristics—including:

■ Purchasing patterns (where and how they shop)

_____

■ Hobbies

_____

■ Recreational activities

_____

■ Publications/media read/watched

_____

■ Social/political philosophy (that is, conservative/liberal)

_____

■ Orientation to technology (that is, technophobe/early adopter)

_____

■ Other

_____

RESEARCHING A TARGET MARKET

FREE RESOURCES

▥ U.S. Census Bureau

Access at: *www.census.gov*

The **U.S. Census Bureau** provides the most comprehensive body of demographic information for target market research. Many companies and nonprofits that provide target market research and demographic data rely to some extent on census data.

The **Census Bureau** provides useful summaries of the most requested data and enables access to it through several user-friendly avenues, including **American FactFinder**, **County Business Patterns**, the **International Data Base**, and **State & County QuickFacts.** All of these sites, plus the home page for **FedStats**, can be accessed through the **U.S. Census Bureau** home page.

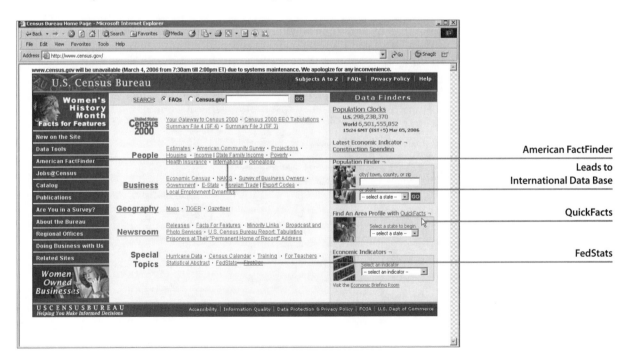

■ U.S. Census Bureau: American FactFinder

Access at: *http://factfinder.census.gov*

Overview: American FactFinder is an excellent easy-to-use online resource for finding comprehensive demographic data at the national, state, county, and even zip code level. The data is presented in a variety of formats, from web pages and PDF documents to detailed, color-coded maps that enable you to zero in on a particular locality.

Best for: Honing in on local target market demographic information.

SAMPLE SEARCHES

A. This search will find the concentration of college graduates in a particular Indianapolis zip code.

1. On the **FactFinder** home page, under **Fast Access to Information**, enter the zip code within which you want to search (in this case, *46201*.)

2. Click **Go**.

1. Enter zip code.

2. Click *Go.*

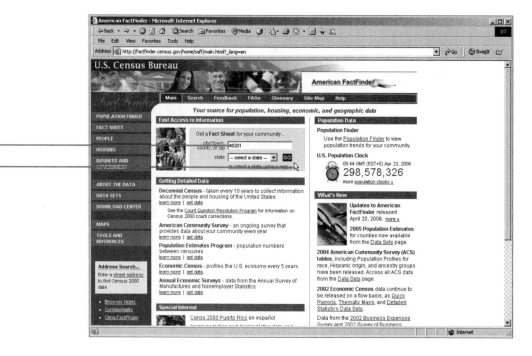

This takes you to a detailed Fact Sheet on the zip code community, featuring data on general, social, economic and housing characteristics.

3. On the **Fact Sheet**, under **Social Characteristics**, find **Bachelor's degree or higher**.

4. Move your cursor across the page along the same row and click **map**.

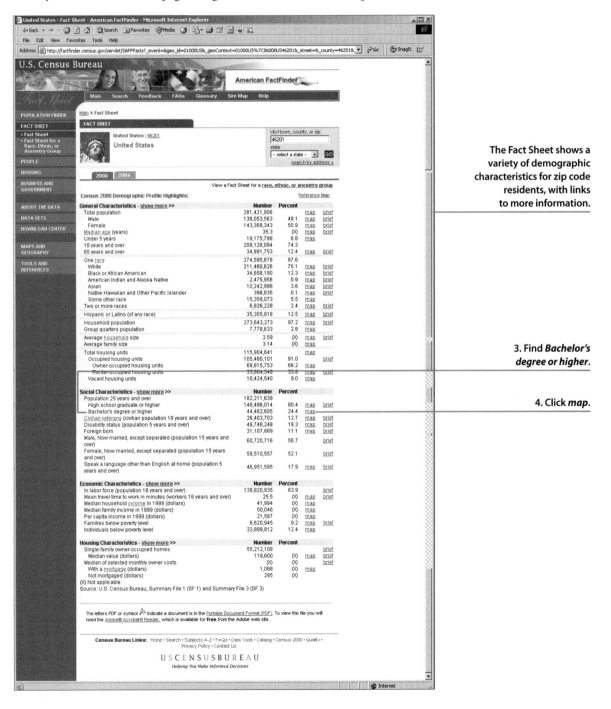

The Fact Sheet shows a variety of demographic characteristics for zip code residents, with links to more information.

3. Find *Bachelor's degree or higher*.

4. Click *map*.

Result: The site presents a map representation of the zip code area highlighting the number of residents with Bachelor's degrees or higher.

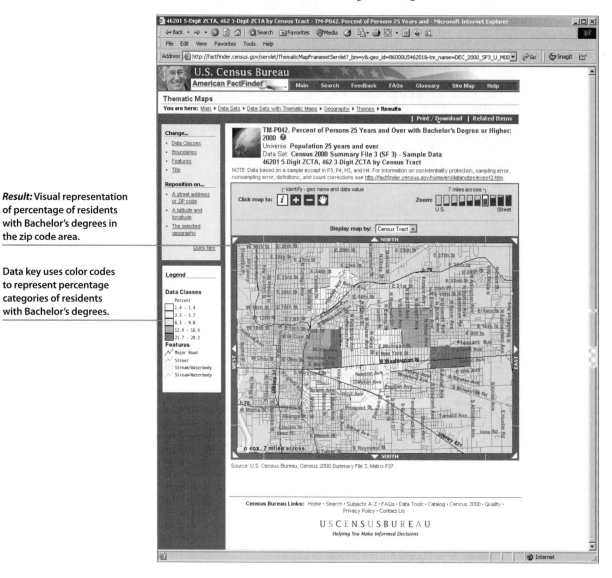

Result: Visual representation of percentage of residents with Bachelor's degrees in the zip code area.

Data key uses color codes to represent percentage categories of residents with Bachelor's degrees.

B. To compare the education levels in your selected zip code with that in other counties and throughout the state, use the **back** button on your Web browser to return to the **Fact Sheet** window.

1. Scroll down to **Social Characteristics**. Under it, find **High school graduate or higher**, then move your cursor across to the **brief** link in the same row.

2. Click **brief**.

1. Find *High school graduate or higher* category.

2. Click *brief* in the same row.

Shows number of high school and college graduates.

This retrieves a twelve-page PDF report detailing Census Bureau data on education levels in the county.

3. Scroll down the report to find state-level education characteristics.

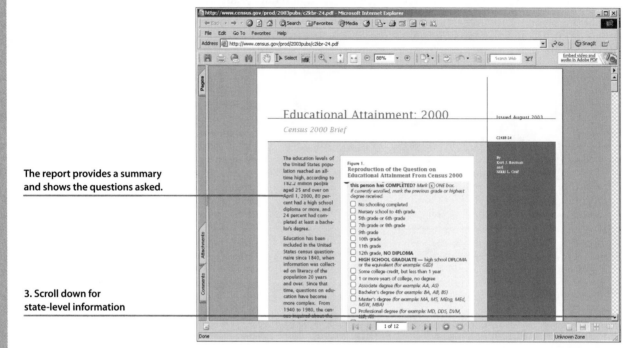

The report provides a summary and shows the questions asked.

3. Scroll down for state-level information

Result: The state-level report provides data on various levels of education in each state by population, from high school graduates to advanced degree holders.

Education level categories (high school to advanced degrees).

Result: **Percentage of state population at each education level.**

Scroll further down the report to find a map showing the percentages of the population with Bachelor's degrees by state and county.

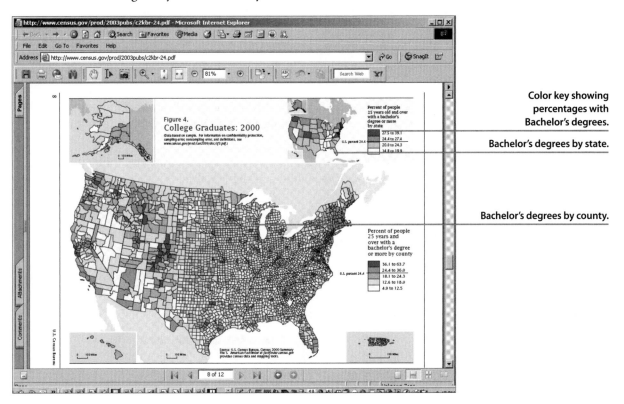

Color key showing percentages with Bachelor's degrees.

Bachelor's degrees by state.

Bachelor's degrees by county.

■ U.S. Census Bureau: County Business Patterns

Access at: *www.census.gov/epcd/cbp/view/cbpview.html*

Overview: With this tool, you can hone in on industry activity within a particular U.S. region—state, county, city, and zip code. Data includes the number of establishments in an area and provides annual economic performance over several years, so you can gauge changes over time. This information can be useful for assessing an industry's viability in a particular geographic location.

Best for: Uncovering local economic data for industries.

SAMPLE SEARCH

This search will reveal the number and size of computer training establishments in Indiana in the year 2003.

1. Scroll down to the list of bulleted links in the middle of the **County Business Patterns** home page.

1. Scroll down to the bulleted links (shown in next image).

2. From the list, select **View County, State, U.S., ZIP, or MSA Database on a NAICS Basis (1998 - 2003)**.

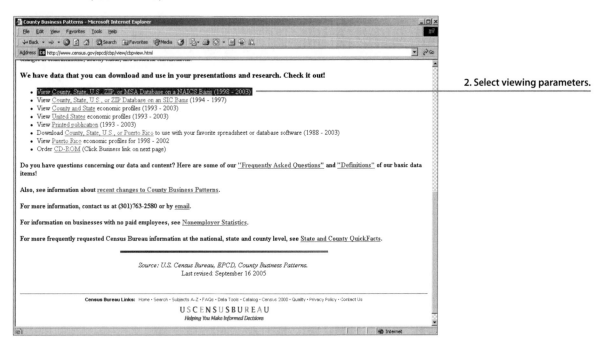

2. Select viewing parameters.

The page that follows gives you the option of searching by state or zip code.

3. From the pull-down menu, select the desired state (in this case, **Indiana**).

4. Click **Go**.

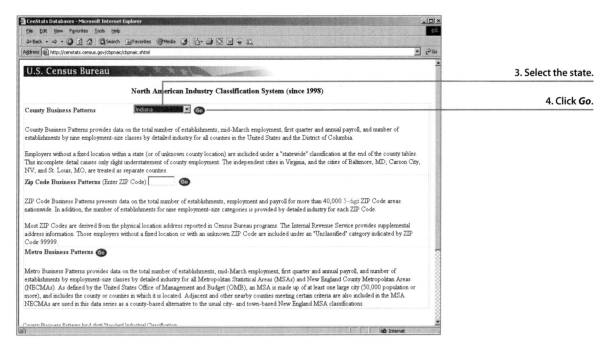

3. Select the state.

4. Click *Go*.

5. On the next page, use the pull-down menu to select the county in Indianapolis that you want to investigate (Marion County).

6. Click **Submit**.

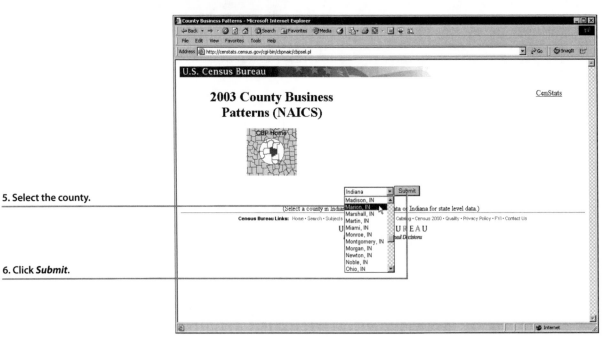

5. Select the county.

6. Click *Submit*.

Result: Data on the number and size (in number of employees) of all the different types of establishments in Marion County.

7. Scroll down to **Educational services**.

8. Click the **Detail** button to the left of the category.

Detail	Compare	31----	Manufacturing	55,706	751,297	2,966,148	1,047
Detail	Compare	42----	Wholesale trade	30,646	343,009	1,369,270	1,779
Detail	Compare	44----	Retail trade	55,293	293,256	1,207,328	3,278
Detail	Compare	48----	Transportation & warehousing	34,753	261,391	1,037,044	663
Detail	Compare	51----	Information	14,221	193,902	745,584	541
Detail	Compare	52----	Finance & insurance	36,861	551,169	2,019,345	1,932
Detail	Compare	53----	Real estate & rental & leasing	12,285	100,801	408,257	1,171
Detail	Compare	54----	Professional, scientific & technical services	34,429	473,249	1,923,015	2,759
Detail	Compare	55----	Management of companies & enterprises	15,830	378,410	1,465,572	202
Detail	Compare	56----	Admin, support, waste mgt, remediation services	40,516	233,066	1,014,862	1,306
Detail	Compare	61----	Educational services	8,557	58,539	223,564	250
Detail	Compare	62----	Health care and social assistance	75,150	671,788	2,800,787	2,358
Detail	Compare	71----	Arts, entertainment & recreation	9,028	95,076	385,630	305
Detail	Compare	72----	Accommodation & food services	45,971	144,932	595,058	1,982
Detail	Compare	81----	Other services (except public administration)	29,877	180,656	735,581	2,575
Detail	Compare	99----	Unclassified establishments	67	232	1,214	48

				Number of Establishments by Employment-size class						
	Industry Code	Industry Code Description	Total Estabs	1-4	5-9	10-19	20-49	50-99	100-249	250-499	500-999	1000 or more

7. Scroll to Educational services.

8. Click Detail.

Result: Data on the number and size of the different types of establishments in Marion County.

The **Marion County Educational Services** page appears, presenting subdivisions of the category.

9. Scroll down to find **Computer Training**.

9. Scroll down to find **Computer Training**.

Result: A report showing the number and size (in number of employees) of computer training establishments in Marion County.

10. For additional information, click the **Compare** button.

10. Click *Compare* for more information.

Result: A report showing the number and size of computer training establishments in Marion County.

Result: The page that appears compares the data on Marion County's computer training establishments with that of other Indiana counties. Marion has more computer training companies than any other county. (This indicates a demand for services there, but it could also mean more competition.)

	FIPS Code	Area Name	Number of Employees for week including March 12	Payroll ($1,000)		Total Establishments	Number of Establishments by Employment-size class								
				1st Quarter	Annual		1-4	5-9	10-19	20-49	50-99	100-249	250-499	500-999	1000 or more
Detail	003	Allen, IN	20-99	0	0	4	2	2	0	0	0	0	0	0	0
Detail	005	Bartholomew, IN	0-19	0	0	2	1	1	0	0	0	0	0	0	0
Detail	011	Boone, IN	0-19	0	0	1	1	0	0	0	0	0	0	0	0
Detail	017	Cass, IN	0-19	0	0	1	1	0	0	0	0	0	0	0	0
Detail	019	Clark, IN	20-99	0	0	1	0	0	0	1	0	0	0	0	0
Detail	025	Crawford, IN	0-19	0	0	1	1	0	0	0	0	0	0	0	0
Detail	029	Dearborn, IN	0-19	0	0	2	2	0	0	0	0	0	0	0	0
Detail	049	Fulton, IN	0-19	0	0	1	1	0	0	0	0	0	0	0	0
Detail	053	Grant, IN	0-19	0	0	1	1	0	0	0	0	0	0	0	0
Detail	057	Hamilton, IN	20-99	0	0	3	2	0	0	1	0	0	0	0	0
Detail	089	Lake, IN	15	74	449	3	2	0	1	0	0	0	0	0	0
Detail	097	Marion, IN	57	475	1,789	12	8	2	2	0	0	0	0	0	0
Detail	099	Marshall, IN	0-19	0	0	1	0	1	0	0	0	0	0	0	0
Detail	127	Porter, IN	20-99	0	0	2	0	0	2	0	0	0	0	0	0
Detail	141	St. Joseph, IN	20-99	0	0	3	1	1	0	1	0	0	0	0	0
Detail	163	Vanderburgh, IN	0-19	0	0	1	1	0	0	0	0	0	0	0	0
Detail	173	Warrick, IN	0-19	0	0	1	1	0	0	0	0	0	0	0	0

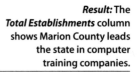

Result: The *Total Establishments* column shows Marion County leads the state in computer training companies.

■ U.S. Census Bureau: International Data Base

Access at: *www.census.gov/ipc/www/idbnew.html* or through the Census Bureau home page at *www.census.gov*.

Overview: This resource provides worldwide demographic and socioeconomic data from 227 countries and areas (including the U.S.).

Best for: Finding international statistics, including population projections.

SAMPLE SEARCH

The goal of this sample search is to find growth projections for China's female population.

1. From the **International Data Base** home page, click on **Summary Demographic Data**.

1. Click *Summary Demographic Data*.

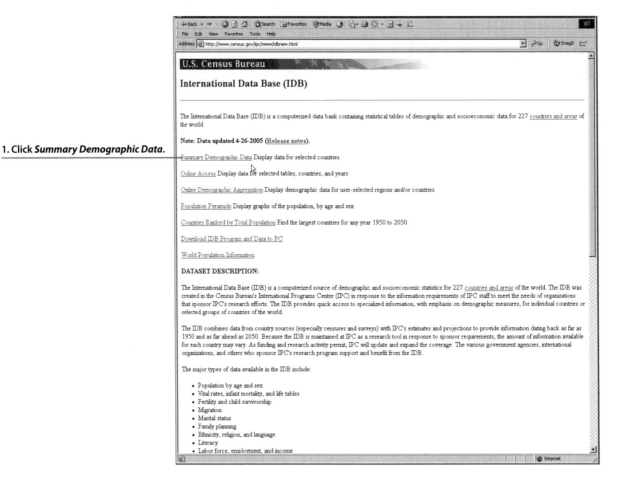

2. On the search page that appears, use the scroll-down menu to select **China**.

3. Click the **Submit Query** button below the menu.

2. Scroll to and select *China*.

3. Click *Submit Query*.

Result: A demographic data report on China, complete with population growth projections.

Result: A demographic
data report on China.

U.S. Census Bureau

IDB Summary Demographic Data for China

Demographic Indicators: 2005 and 2025

	2005	2025
Births per 1,000 population....................	13	11
Deaths per 1,000 population....................	7	8
Rate of natural increase (percent).............	0.6	0.2
Annual rate of growth (percent)...............	0.6	0.2
Life expectancy at birth (years)...............	72.3	77.2
Infant deaths per 1,000 live births............	24	11
Total fertility rate (per woman)..............	1.7	1.8

Midyear Population Estimates and Average Annual Period Growth Rates:
1950 to 2050
         (Population in thousands, rate in percent)

Year	Population	Year	Population	Period	Growth Rate
1950	562,580	2005	1,306,314	1950-1960	1.5
1960	650,661	2006	1,313,974	1960-1970	2.3
1970	820,403	2007	1,321,852	1970-1980	1.8
1980	984,736	2008	1,330,045	1980-1990	1.5
1990	1,148,364	2009	1,338,613	1990-2000	1.0
2000	1,268,853	2010	1,347,563	2000-2010	0.6
2001	1,276,882	2020	1,430,533	2010-2020	0.6
2002	1,284,276	2030	1,461,528	2020-2030	0.2
2003	1,291,496	2040	1,454,619	2030-2040	0.0
2004	1,298,848	2050	1,424,162	2040-2050	-0.2

4. Scroll down the page to find population growth projections by gender.

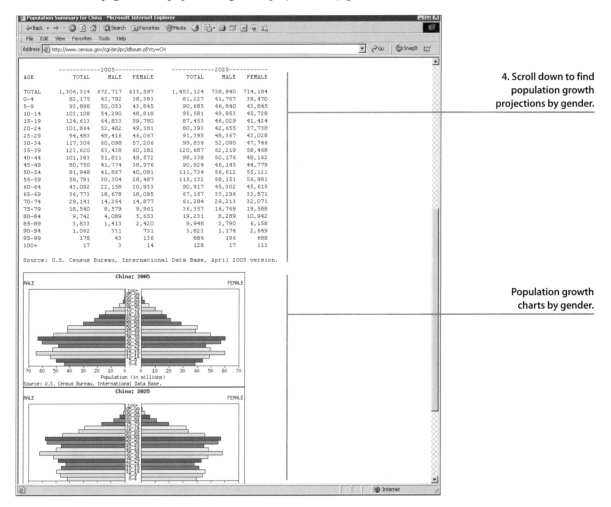

4. Scroll down to find population growth projections by gender.

Population growth charts by gender.

■ U.S. Census Bureau: State & County QuickFacts

Access at: *http://quickfacts.census.gov* or through the U.S. Census Bureau home page at *www.census.gov*.

Overview: This Census Bureau resource features summaries of the most-requested demographic information for states and counties. Data includes population characteristics such as age, education, and income levels.

Best for: State and county demographic data.

SAMPLE SEARCH

Here is a sample search to determine education levels in Indianapolis, Indiana.

1. Use the pull-down menu on the QuickFacts home page to choose the state for which you need data (in this case, **Indiana**).

2. Click **Go**.

Alternatively, you can use the map on this page to click on the state of Indiana, which takes you to the same place as the pull-down menu (the **Indiana QuickFacts** page).

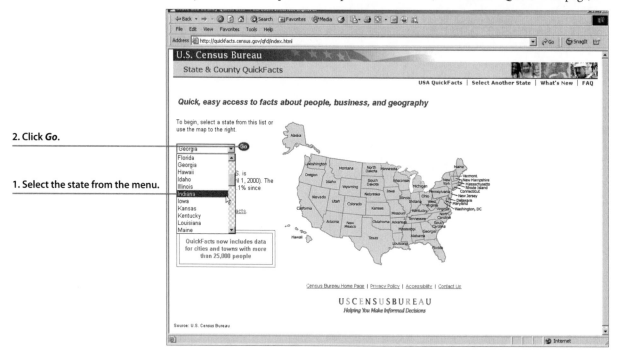

2. Click *Go*.

1. Select the state from the menu.

The **Indiana QuickFacts** section presents a comprehensive page of data on the people living in the state.

3. To narrow your search, use the pull-down menus at the top of the page to select your county or city. (**Indianapolis** is selected here).

4. Click **Go**.

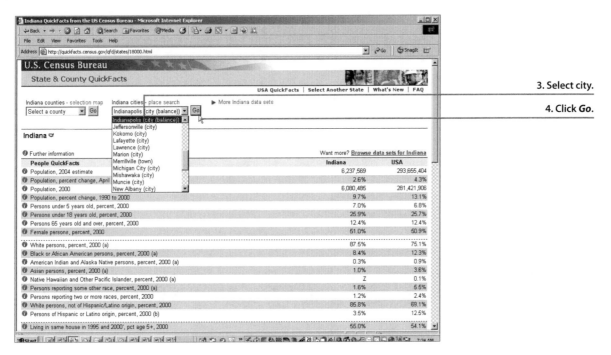

3. Select city.

4. Click *Go*.

This retrieves the city of Indianapolis QuickFacts page, which shows the same data categories as the state-level page.

5. Scroll down the page to find relevant data on education levels in the city.

5. Scroll down to find education data.

Result: Relevant statistics on education levels in Indianapolis, compared to state levels.

Result: Statistics on education levels in Indianapolis.

	Indianapolis	Indiana
Living in same house in 1995 and 2000', pct age 5+, 2000	47.3%	55.0%
Foreign born persons, percent, 2000	4.6%	3.1%
Language other than English spoken at home, pct age 5+, 2000	7.3%	6.4%
High school graduates, percent of persons age 25+, 2000	81.3%	82.1%
Bachelor's degree or higher, pct of persons age 25+, 2000	25.4%	19.4%
Mean travel time to work (minutes), workers age 16+, 2000	22.7	22.6
Housing units, 2000	352,429	2,532,319
Homeownership rate, 2000	58.6%	71.4%
Median value of owner-occupied housing units, 2000	$98,200	$94,300
Households, 2000	320,107	2,336,306
Persons per household, 2000	2.39	2.53
Median household income, 1999	$40,051	$41,567
Per capita money income, 1999	$21,640	$20,397
Persons below poverty, percent, 1999	11.9%	9.5%
Business QuickFacts	**Indianapolis**	**Indiana**
Manufacturers shipments, 1997 ($1000)	17,918,825	11,300,008
Wholesale trade sales, 1997 ($1000)	D	66,350,132
Retail sales, 1997 ($1000)	10,228,013	57,241,650
Retail sales per capita, 1997	$13,751	$9,748
Accomodation and foodservices sales, 1997 ($1000)	1,448,463	6,646,318
Total number of firms, 1997	57,322	413,400
Minority-owned firms, percent of total, 1997	11.3%	5.5%
Women-owned firms, percent of total, 1997	25.8%	25.9%
Geography QuickFacts	**Indianapolis**	**Indiana**
Land area, 2000 (square miles)	361	35,867
Persons per square mile, 2000	2,163.0	169.5
FIPS Code	36003	18
Counties	Marion County	

Download delimited tables | Download Excel tables

6. For additional statistics on Indianapolis, click **Browse data sets for Indianapolis**, located above the first statistics column.

6. Click for more stats.

Result: This retrieves a page of useful QuickLinks to statistics on Indianapolis.

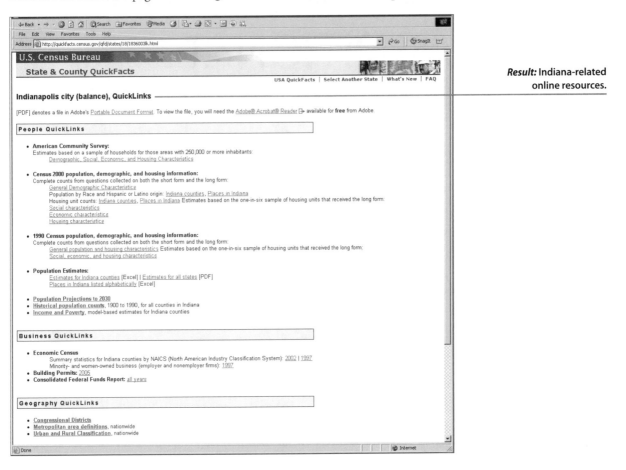

Result: Indiana-related
online resources.

RESEARCHING A TARGET MARKET

ADDITIONAL FREE RESOURCES

■ FedStats

Access at: *www.fedstats.gov*

Overview: FedStats provides a powerful service for leveraging demographic data collected from more than one hundred federal agencies. Its MapStats subsection uses Census data, organized in a similar fashion to that retrieved through the QuickFacts interface.

Best for: Finding a variety of federal data on U.S. and international demographics organized into one comprehensive resource.

■ RDS TableBase

Access at: Public and college/university libraries.

Overview: In addition to providing numerical data for industry research (see listing in the *Industry* section, page 102), **TableBase** offers data and articles on demographics, market trends, and consumer-related information. Sources include statistical annuals, trade association reports, non-profit research groups, international organizations, and government agencies.

Best for: Finding numerical and chart-based demographic data.

■ Sperling's BestPlaces

Access at: *www.bestplaces.net*

Overview: Bestplaces.net is an easy-to-navigate site for comprehensive information on county, city, and neighborhood demographics across the U.S. The profiles include snapshots of local economies, housing, health, crime, climate, education, transportation, and cost of living as well as hard-to-find breakdowns of an area's religious affiliations by percentage of population. Click on Zip Profiles at the top of the home page to access profiles of all U.S. zip codes.

Best for: Searching for demographic information by zip code.

RESEARCHING A TARGET MARKET

FEE-BASED RESOURCES

■ Community Sourcebook America

Access at: College/university libraries (on CD-ROM).

Overview: Community Sourcebook America enables you to gauge consumer spending patterns by geographic area (such as state, county, and zip code). You can compare spending for twenty key products and services ranging from home improvements to take-out food. Data on spending levels is measured by the Spending Patterns Index (SPI). Generally the geographic areas that score higher on the index spend more on the items in question. The **Sourcebook** provides an easy guide on how to interpret the index numbers.

You can also view spending patterns in different categories using detailed visual maps accessed through the **Sourcebook** window. The maps allow you to quickly compare spending from one geographic region to another. This could help you determine the best market for a particular product or service.

Best for: Finding localized target market spending data by geographic region.

Part IV: STRAIGHT TO THE NUMBERS YOU NEED

SAMPLE SEARCH

The search will uncover general spending characteristics for the residents of Marion County, Indiana, and reveal how their spending on computers and hardware compares to that in neighboring counties.

1. Start at the opening title window. This will appear briefly before presenting the search box.

1. Title window appears briefly before presenting the search box.

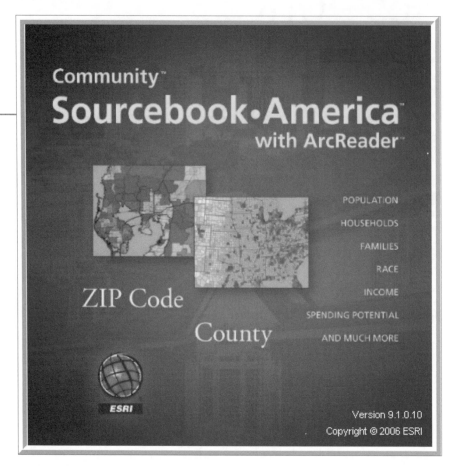

When the title screen fades, the **New Project** box appears.

2. Under **Available Databases** in the left-hand column, select **County**.

3. In the right column, under **Select by Geographic Level**, choose the **County** option. A list of counties throughout the U.S. will appear.

4. Scroll down to select the county that interests you (in this case, **Marion, IN**.)

5. Click **OK**.

New Project

Available Data Series [Location]: 2005 Edition [E:\ ]

Available Databases

| CBSA |
| County |
| County Business Data |
| DMA |
| Nonresidential ZIP Code |
| State |
| US |
| ZIP Code |
| ZIP Code Business Data |
| ZIP Code Tapestry |

Select by Geographic Level
- ○ State   ● County
- ○ CBSA

| 18085 - Kosciusko, IN |
| 18087 - LaGrange, IN |
| 18089 - Lake, IN |
| 18091 - LaPorte, IN |
| 18093 - Lawrence, IN |
| 18095 - Madison, IN |
| 18097 - Marion, IN |
| 18099 - Marshall, IN |
| 18101 - Martin, IN |
| 18103 - Miami, IN |
| 18105 - Monroe, IN |
| 18107 - Montgomery, IN |
| 18109 - Morgan, IN |
| 18111 - Newton, IN |

Help   Cancel   OK

2. Select the *County* database.

3. Select *County* geographic level.

4. Select the appropriate county from the list that appears.

5. Click *OK*.

Data for the selected county will appear.

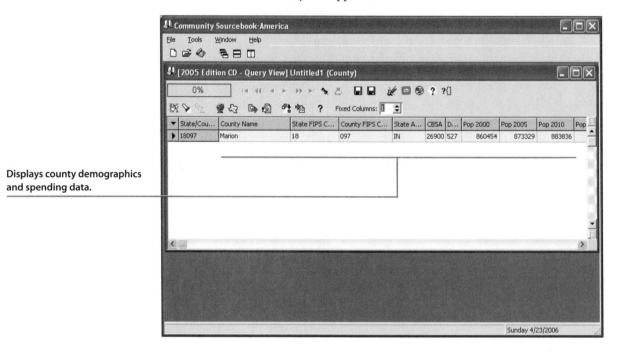

Displays county demographics and spending data.

6. Scroll *across* to the **Spending Potential Index** in a variety of consumer areas such as investments, travel, apparel, and pet supplies. (*Note:* The median is 100.)

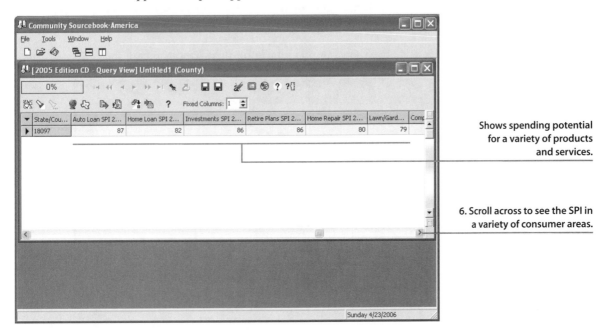

Shows spending potential for a variety of products and services.

6. Scroll across to see the SPI in a variety of consumer areas.

7. Using the pull-down **File** menu at the top of the window, select **View Maps with ArcReader**. A box will appear titled **Select Map to View with ArcReader**.

7. Click on *File* and select *View Maps with ArcReader*.

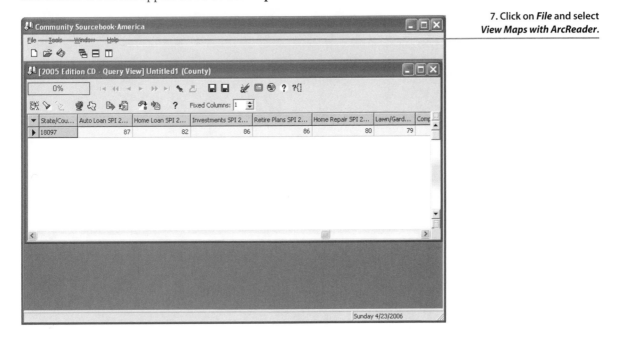

8. Under **Select Geography**, choose **County**.

9. Under **Select Data Item**, choose **Computers and Hardware Spending Potential**.

10. Click the **Show** button in the lower right-hand corner of the box.

8. Select *County* from the pull-down menu.

9. Choose *Computers and Hardware Spending Potential*.

10. Click *Show*.

Select Map to View with ArcReader ☒

Available Data Series [Location]: 2005 Edition [E:\ ] ▾

Select Geography:

County ▾

Select Data Item

Apparel Spending Potential
Auto Loan Spending Potential
Auto Repairs Spending Potential
Average Household Size
Cable TV Spending Potential
Computers and Hardware Spending Potential
Dine In/Carry Out Spending Potential
Families 2000
Families 2005

Help   Close   Show

A national map will appear, with counties designated and spending potential highlighted.

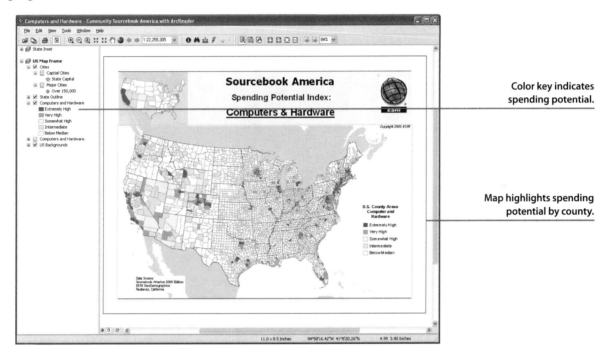

Color key indicates spending potential.

Map highlights spending potential by county.

Zoom in on Marion County to get a visual representation of the spending potential in that market and compare it to surrounding counties.

Result: Based on the levels indicated by the color key in the left-hand column, spending on computers and hardware is extremely high in Marion County.

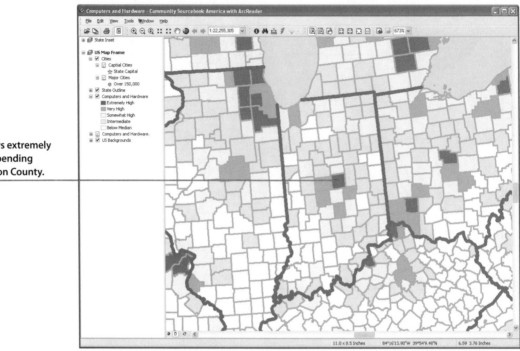

Result: Map shows extremely high computer spending potential in Marion County.

■ Mintel

Access at: *www.mintel.com*; access reports for free through a college or university library. If accessing through a library, take a couple of minutes to create an account so you can store the reports you find or create. If you are not accessing the site through an academic library, you must register to purchase one of these expensive reports.

Overview: This excellent, up-to-date resource provides detailed information on consumer behavior as it relates to a wide range of industries, products, and life stages. For additional information on this resource and another sample search, see page 124.

Best for: Gathering detailed consumer demographic, lifestyle, and psychographic data.

SAMPLE SEARCHES

A. This first sample search will use the reports tab to look for demographic information on young adults living in the U.S.

1. On the home page, click the **reports** tab for a listing of report categories.

1. Click reports tab for report categories.

2. On the **report range** page, click **lifestages**.

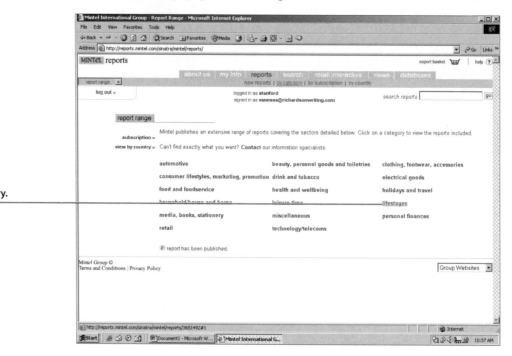

2. Click report category.

3. The page refreshes to show a selection of relevant reports. Select **Lifestyles of Young Adults**.

3. Select the report most likely to contain relevant information.

This retrieves a page that breaks the report down by section.

4. Choose **Demographics of Young Adults**.

4. Choose relevant report section.

Result: A nationwide overview of young adult demographics, including such factors as age, race, household size, employment, and income.

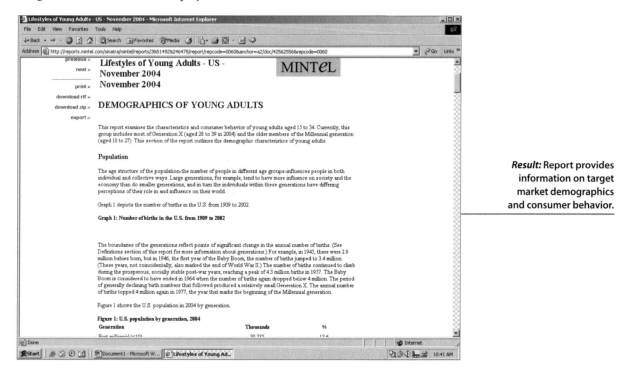

Result: Report provides information on target market demographics and consumer behavior.

B. The second search will seek psychographic (personality-related) data on this same target market, young adults living in the U.S.

1. Return to the home page and click the **my info** tab.

1. Click the *my info* tab.

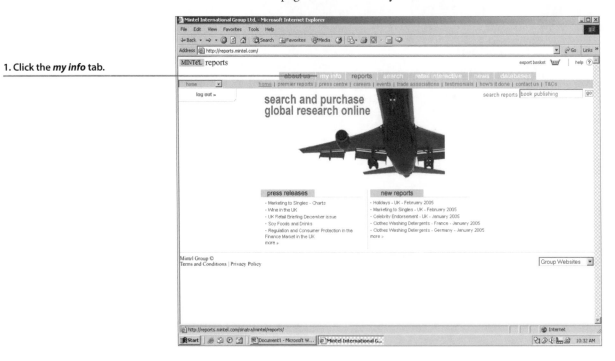

The next page presents another list of reports, divided into new categories.

2. Select **US Lifestyles**.

2. Select a relevant category.

The lifestyle reports listed provide a host of psychographic information about your target market, including their attitudes, habits, activities, and spending patterns.

3. Choose **Lifestyles of Young Adults** from the list.

3. Choose the report most likely to provide relevant behavioral data on your target market.

Part IV: STRAIGHT TO THE NUMBERS YOU NEED

Result: The "Executive Summary" of the report offers a wide range of lifestyle information on the young adult market, from a demographic analysis to information on spending patterns.

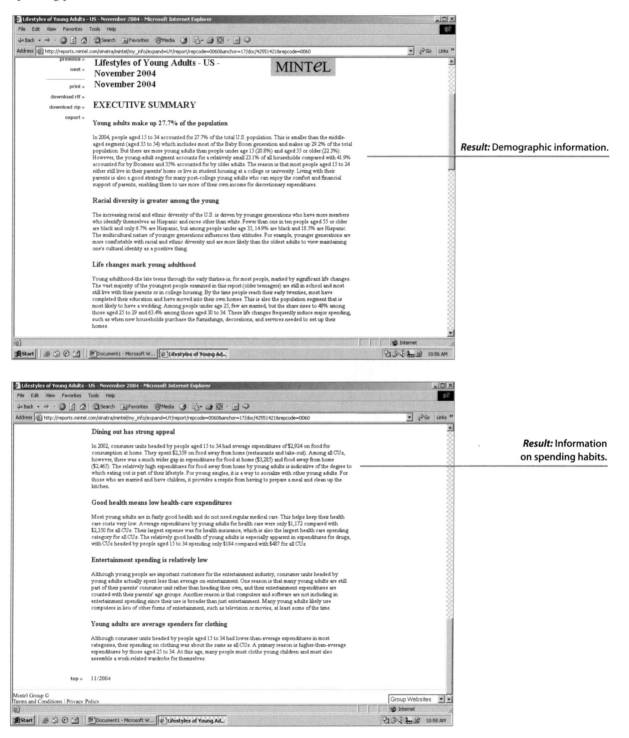

Result: Demographic information.

Result: Information on spending habits.

■ MarketResearch.com Academic

Access at: *www.marketresearch.com* (*Note:* Reports accessed through the site can cost thousands of dollars) or for free through college/university libraries.

Overview: MarketResearch.com offers consumer, industry, demographic, and lifestyle-oriented reports designed to help companies create their marketing strategies. In addition to comprehensive analysis, these reports contain charts, tables, graphs, and key facts about the topic area.

Best for: Finding demographic and lifestyle reports.

SAMPLE SEARCH

This search will look for information related to baby boomers and computer usage.

1. On the home page, enter relevant keywords (*computer education*) in the search field on the left-hand side of the page. (*Note:* The keywords *computer training* retrieved no relevant results.)

2. Click **Go** to retrieve results.

1. Enter search terms.

2. Click *Go* to get results.

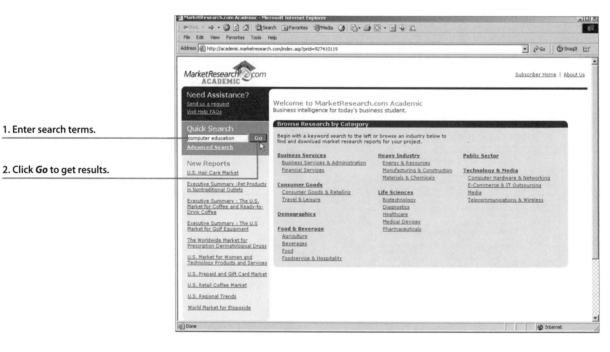

The search retrieves a number of articles on computer education for various demographic groups.

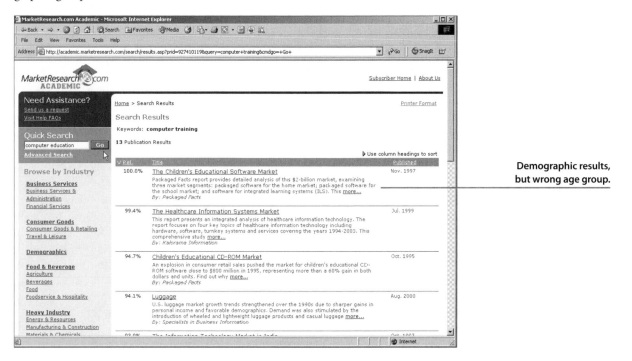

Demographic results, but wrong age group.

3. Scroll down the page to view the results.

An article on consumers aged 55+ shows promise, as that group accounts for part of the baby boomer generation.

4. Click the article title.

3. Scroll down the page to view results.

4. Click article on baby boomer age group.

This takes you to an abstract of the article, which gives you the opportunity to view the table of contents.

5. Click **Table of Contents**.

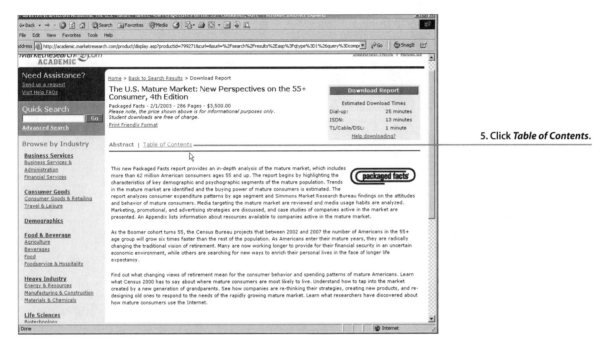

5. Click *Table of Contents*.

6. Scroll through the contents to find topics related to computer training for this age group in the Indianapolis region.

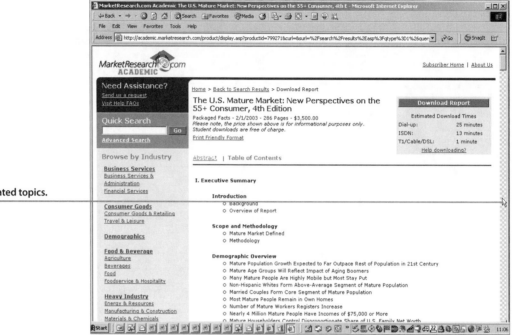

6. Scroll to find related topics.

As indicated below, the content shows at least two items that would be of interest when looking for data on computer education for older adults in Indianapolis.

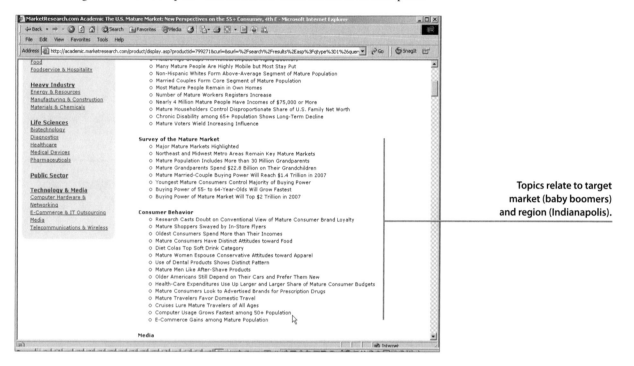

Topics relate to target market (baby boomers) and region (Indianapolis).

7. To get a copy of the full report, click **Download Report** in the upper right-hand corner.

8. You will be prompted with a box asking if you want to save the report to your computer or open it. (It's usually better to save it on your computer than to open it from the website.)

7. Click *Download Report*.

8. When box appears, save the report and open it from your computer.

Result: A PDF version of a report that includes information on growing computer usage among senior baby boomers and on baby boomers in the northern Midwest region the U.S.

(*Note:* One drawback of this site is the lack of information on file size of the reports to be downloaded. The Download Report box gives time estimates for different types of Internet connections, but this sample search found those times to be inaccurate.)

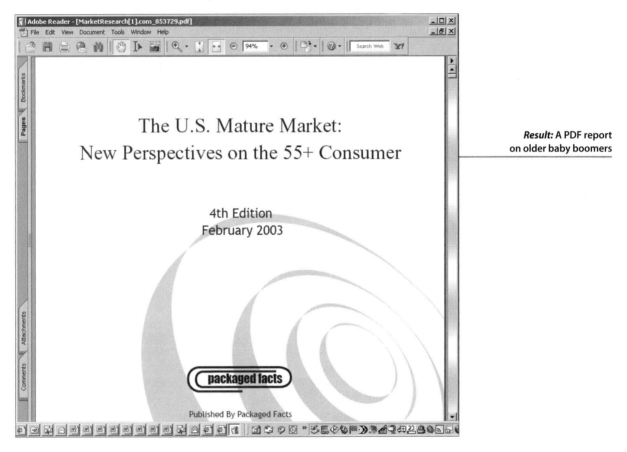

Result: A PDF report on older baby boomers

RESEARCHING A TARGET MARKET

ADDITIONAL FEE-BASED RESOURCES

■ American Demographics Magazine

Access at: *www.demographics.com*

Overview: *American Demographics* magazine posts weekly articles on how specific trends, issues, and events shape consumer market segments and buying behavior. Articles cover a broad range of topics from "Understanding the 'Generation Wireless' Demographic" to "No-Haggle Pricing Climbs Higher." This site requires you to register to access articles. Articles are free for the first seven days, but after that you will be charged a small fee per article.

Best for: Gathering information on consumer buying trends.

■ Choices 3

Access at: College/university libraries in CD-ROM format.

Overview: Choices 3 is a CD-ROM version of the Simmons National Consumer Survey (NCS) database, which holds detailed data on consumers' buying and media behavior patterns. All data is based on Simmons survey responses of adults aged eighteen and older from over 30,000 U.S. households. You can use this tool to create customized, cross-tabulated reports for a wide variety of products and consumers' demographic (age, sex, marital status, household, education, etc.) and lifestyle profiles. You can also cross-tabulate data on consumers' demographic characteristics and their media habits (what newspapers and magazines they read, TV channels they watch, and radio stations they listen to).

Best for: Creating demographic and psychographic profiles of consumers to identify likely customers and the best way to reach them.

◾ Mediamark Reporter

Access at: College/university libraries in CD-ROM format.

Overview: This tool shows you what types of consumers are most likely to buy certain products or services and what marketing approaches are best to reach them. **Mediamark** surveys 25,000 U.S. consumers aged eighteen and older, gathering information on product usage /consumption, lifestyle, and media preferences (what they watch, listen to, and read). Data for more than 450 categories and 6,000 brands is collected on its CD-ROM software. (*Note:* The **Mediamark** information available at some libraries may not contain the most recent data.)

Best for: Discovering the purchasing habits, lifestyle preferences, and other behavioral traits of consumers.

◾ Stat-USA

Access at: *www.stat-usa.gov*

Overview: This subscription-based service, available through the U.S. Department of Commerce, provides access to federal business, economic and trade data. According to the website, the Department charges a $200 annual subscription fee for government data mainly to cover the costs of better service and improvements in their technology. The global feature of this service is particularly good for finding information on international markets. This site is better for sophisticated researchers. Casual business researchers may find it confusing.

Best for: Finding sophisticated U.S. and international market research.

Glossary of Business and Research Terms

Annual payroll: All forms of compensation, including salaries, wages, commissions, bonuses, vacation pay, sick pay, and employer contributions to pension plans.

Boolean search: A system of search logic that uses three primary operators, **AND**, **OR**, and **NOT**, to filter information. On search engines, these three operators are used with keywords to broaden or narrow a search, and must be entered in upper case to set off their functionality. See also **Proximity search**.

Business-to-consumer (B-to-C): A business that targets and sells its products and/or services to a consumer market (rather than to other businesses).

Business-to-business (B-to-B): A business that targets and sells its products to other businesses (rather than to consumers).

Data: While used interchangeably with *information* in this book, the term often implies numerical information. See also **Information**.

Database: An organized collection of resources, information, and statistical data stored in one or more computerized files and retrieved in a systematic manner.

Demographics: Characteristics that define a group of people, such as age, sex, income and education. Often used in statistical analysis of a population.

Establishment (as defined by the U.S. Census Bureau): A business entity operating from a single physical location (as opposed to a company or enterprise, which may have multiple locations). See also **Firm**.

Firm (as defined by the U.S. Census Bureau): Synonymous with *company*. A business entity with one or more establishments (locations) under common ownership or control. See also **Establishment**.

Industry: Defined broadly here to mean an economic sector (such as manufacturing), a broad business type (such as clothing manufacturing), or a very specific business type (such as sporting goods or clothing retail stores). The U.S. Census Bureau, by contrast, more narrowly defines *industry* as an entity classified under a 5- or 6-digit NAICS code. See also **North American Industry Classification System (NAICS)**.

Information: Data, facts, analysis and other material sought through research. See also **Data**.

Margin of error: A measurement of a survey's accuracy. A large margin of error suggests a less accurate survey; a small margin of error implies a more accurate one. In relation to sampling, the margin of error shows the extent to which the survey results reflect (or deviate from) the characteristics of the larger population. See also **Sampling**.

North American Industry Classification System (NAICS): A standard industry classification method currently used by the governments of the United States, Canada, and Mexico. See also **Standard Industry Classification System (SIC)**.

Primary research: Original research requiring direct contact with your research subjects (such as target customers). See also **Secondary research**.

Proximity search: A system of search logic that uses the terms **NEAR**, **BEFORE**, and **AFTER** to specify how close words should be to each other, or where they should appear in relation to each other in the results. Some search engines require the use of the terms (capitalized to set off their functionality); others use this logic by default, based on the ordering of the words. See also **Boolean search**.

Psychographics: Psychological characteristics, traits, and lifestyle practices used to describe consumers.

Resource (as used in this book): A website, database, search engine, or other research tool that allows researchers to find sources and other information quickly and efficiently. (*Note:* Resources described in this book are all websites and databases.) See also **Source**.

Revenues: Gross sales; all pre-tax money received from doing business, except for sales taxes and other taxes collected from customers.

Qualitative research: Research based on observations of characteristics, as opposed to numerical data. Qualitative studies are usually conducted by interviewing, surveying, or observing research subjects (such as target market consumers) and often seek subjective responses (for example, a verbal or written response in an opinion poll). See also **Quantitative research**.

Quantitative research: Research that relies on numerical data, such as statistics and numerical measures of characteristics (examples include revenue figures, population data, an opinion poll that asks respondents to rate the value of an item on a 1-to-10 scale). See also **Qualitative research**.

Sampling: A set of subjects or respondents in a study. The usually random selection (for research purposes) of a group of people whose characteristics are deemed representative of a larger population. See also **Margin of Error**.

Secondary Research: Research that requires no contact with research subjects, but relies on data from primary researchers. See also **Primary research**.

Sector (as defined by the U.S. Census Bureau): Entities that fall under the 2-digit NAICS classification system (composed of different industry subsectors). See also **Subsector**.

Source (as used in this book): An entity that has gathered and/or provided the information you seek in the form of a document or another piece of data. You can use the resources in this book to find specific sources. (Example: The researcher used LexisNexis Ala Carte!, a resource, to locate an article in Market Share Reporter, a source. See also **Resource**.

Standard Industry Classification System (SIC): A system of industry classification no longer used or revised by the U.S. government. The North American Industry Classification System (NAICS) replaced SIC in an effort to standardize classifications and statistical data between the North American nations and to accommodate new types of emerging industries. However, many resources still allow for searching by SIC codes and sources still refer to them. See also **North American Industry Classification System (NAICS)**.

Subsector (as defined by the U.S. Census Bureau): Entities that fall under the 3-digit NAICS classifications (composed of sets of industries). See also **Sector**.

Index

Acknowledgments

The Planning Shop and Rhonda Abrams would like to thank:

Maggie Canon, Managing Editor. Maggie brings an outstanding background in the publishing industry to her position with The Planning Shop. She was founding editor of *InfoWorld* and numerous other technology magazines and was also managing editor of the bestselling *America 24/7* series. Maggie's energy, professionalism, and intelligence have been an invaluable addition to the Planning Shop.

Mireille Majoor, Editorial Project Manager, who oversees the editorial process of this and every The Planning Shop book. She is a consummate professional and both The Planning Shop books and readers have benefited from Mireille's commitment to excellence.

Deborah Kaye, who manages The Planning Shop's relations with the academic community. Deborah's unwavering dedication to the professors and students who use our books and resources have earned her a large group of devoted academic fans. Deborah has been The Planning Shop's guiding light for many years and we are continually appreciative of her contribution.

Rosa Whitten, Office Manager and the newest member of The Planning Shop's team. Rosa comes to us with years of organizational experience. She is already proving to be invaluable—in terms of both her skills and her positive outlook. We are delighted to have her help to guide us.

Arthur Wait, who designed the look and feel of The Planning Shop's line of books and products and developed our website and electronic products. We are always amazed (though no longer surprised) by the range of Arthur's talents.

Diana Van Winkle, who brought her graphic expertise to the design of this book. She is talented, responsive, and a delight to work with. Diana's skills ensure that The Planning Shop's books continue to be easy and pleasurable for readers to use.

Kathryn Dean, who brought her eagle eye to the proofing process, ensuring that our books are pristine and error free.

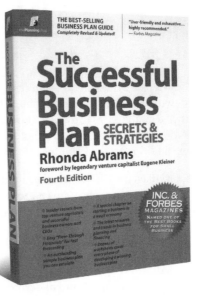